Collins

History for Trinidad and Tobago

Forms 1, 2 & 3

Editors: **Dr Nicole Phillip-Dowe, Eartha Thomas Hunte**

Reviewer: **Shivan Maharaj**

Collins

Published by Collins
HarperCollins*Publishers*
The News Building
1 London Bridge Street
London SE1 9GF

HarperCollins *Publishers*
Macken House,
39/40 Mayor Street Upper,
Dublin 1,
D01 C9W8
Ireland

First edition 2022

10 9 8 7 6 5 4 3 2

ISBN 978-0-00-852812-6

Browse the complete Collins Caribbean catalogue at
www.collins.co.uk/caribbeanschools

A catalogue record for this book is available from the British Library.

If any copyright holders have been omitted, please contact the Publisher, who will make the necessary arrangements at the first opportunity.

Contributors: Keri-Marie Campbell, Lisa Greenstein, Daphne Paizee, Bruce Nicholson, Susie Clarke, Dave Ramsingh
Reviewer: Shivan Maharaj
Series Editors: Nicole Philip-Dowe, Eartha Thomas-Hunte
Publisher: Elaine Higgleton
Commissioning Editor: Bruce Nicholson
Project Management: Oriel Square
Typesetting and layout: Jouve
Cover design: Kevin Robbins and Gordon MacGilp
Cover image: © John de la Bastide/Shutterstock
Maps: Sarah Woods, Gordon MacGilp and Ewan Ross

See also page 120 for photograph acknowledgements.

Printed and bound in the UK using 100% Renewable Electricity at CPI Group (UK) Ltd

Contents

How to use this book

These learning objectives tell you what you will be learning about in the lesson.

Each topic is divided into headings

Activity features allow you to do practical activities related to the topic.

Try these questions to check your understanding of each topic.

The history of my school

We are learning to:
- trace the history of our sources
- collect information through interviews and observations
- work collaboratively to produce a history of our school.

Tracing the history of my school

Some schools in Trinidad and Tobago have long, proud traditions. Your own school may be new or it may have started years ago. The people who started the school will have set out their **vision** for it and considered questions like these:

- What type of school is it and who will attend?
- What will be taught at the school (the **curriculum**)?
- Will the students wear a **uniform** and what will that be? How many students will be admitted?
- Where will the lessons take place? Who will teach the students?
- Will there be **extra-curricular** and sports activities?
- Who will lead the school?

Case study

The Far Hills High School is a landmark in the community. The school was **established** in 1953 and its **rationale** was to empower boys and girls of all religions and races to achieve academic success. The school provided education for children who lived in the area, who had previously had to travel far to attend school.

The school opened with 43 students in four classrooms. The school offered a full academic programme as well as extra-curricular activities such as sports, music and drama. Students from the school have distinguished themselves in many walks of life.

Over the years the school has grown. New classrooms have been added and there are now 450 students.

Questions

1. Why was the Far Hills School set up?
2. Do you think all children in the community were welcomed at this school?
3. Has the Far Hills School been successful in serving its community? Explain your answer.

Activity

Working in pairs, study the photograph of the old school classroom on page 17. Compare this classroom with your own classroom.

Discussion

What do you know about the history of your own school? Discuss the history of your school with your teacher.

16   History for Trinidad and Tobago: The history of my school

Discussion features allow you to work in pairs, in a group or as a class to explore the topic further.

Gathering information about your school

When researching the history of your school, you will need to think about:

- why it was set up and when
- the vision, **mission** and extra-curricular activities
- uniforms, buildings, sports and awards
- the legacy of the school, principal, teachers, students
- customs and traditions of the school.

There are many different ways of finding out about the history of your own school. You can start by observing your school buildings and sources of information at your school. Your school library may have information like this:

- Primary sources such as photographs that show the school at different times
- Copies of old school magazines with photographs and articles about school life during a specific year
- Trophies and honour rolls that record the achievements of students over the years.

Older members of the community can provide interesting information about daily life at school. You can set up interviews with some people. Draw up a questionnaire with questions similar to these:

- Did you attend this school?
- Which subjects did you study?
- Did you do any extra-curricular activities?
- Were you punished if you did not obey rules? How?
- What were your best memories of the school?

Secondary sources such as articles in magazines and newspapers can also provide valuable information about schools. You can search the websites of local newspapers for articles.

Project

Working in groups, and then as a class, produce a booklet about the history of your school. To do this you will need to do some careful planning and then work cooperatively. Everyone in the class should make a contribution.

The information that you collect should come from interviews and other primary and secondary sources. You should also compile a bibliography to acknowledge the sources you have used and create a timeline to show the major events in the school's history.

Did you know...?

In 1825 there were only six schools on the island of Trinidad. One was an English female boarding school, three were French day schools in Port-of-Spain, one school was maintained by the Cabildo for teaching the English language, and a small day school was being operated in an Amerindian village where only Spanish was taught.

Topics have some fascinating extra facts.

Key vocabulary

vision

curriculum (curricula)

uniform

extra-curricular

established

rationale

mission

These are the most important new words in the topic. You can check their meanings in the Glossary at the end of the book.

17

Project features allow you to work on your own or in groups to explore the topic further and present your findings to your class or your teacher.

This page gives a summary of the exciting new ideas you will be learning about in the unit.

These lists at the end of a unit act as a checklist of the key ideas of the unit.

This is the topic covered in the unit, which links to the syllabus.

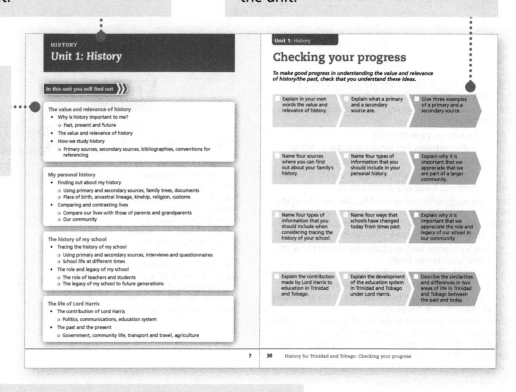

These end-of-unit questions allow you and your teacher to check that you have understood the ideas in Unit 1, and can explain history using the skills and knowledge you have gained.

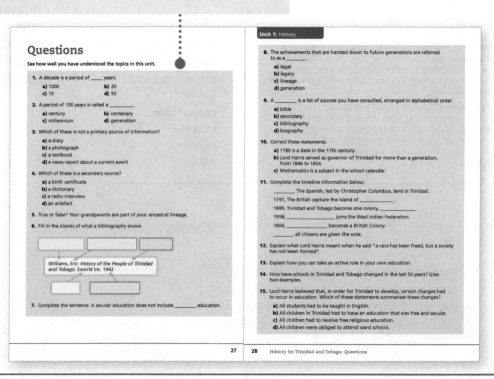

Unit 1: History

In this unit you will find out

The value and relevance of history

- Why is history important to me?
  - ○ Past, present and future
- The value and relevance of history
- How we study history
  - ○ Primary sources, secondary sources, bibliographies, conventions for referencing

My personal history

- Finding out about my history
  - ○ Using primary and secondary sources, family trees, documents
  - ○ Place of birth, ancestral lineage, kinship, religion, customs
- Comparing and contrasting lives
  - ○ Compare our lives with those of parents and grandparents
  - ○ Our community

The history of my school

- Tracing the history of my school
  - ○ Using primary and secondary sources, interviews and questionnaires
  - ○ School life at different times
- The role and legacy of my school
  - ○ The role of teachers and students
  - ○ The legacy of my school to future generations

The life of Lord Harris

- The contribution of Lord Harris
  - ○ Politics, communications, education system
- The past and the present
  - ○ Government, community life, transport and travel, agriculture

The value and relevance of history

We are learning to:

- define and use correctly the terms past, present, future, decade, century, generation
- describe the value and relevance of history to myself and my country.

Why is history important to me? 〉〉

History is the study of the past. Most of us are so involved with our modern world that we forget to stop and think about the past. Yet, how can we really understand who we are if we do not value our past? Our understanding of history helps us to understand the present, and to understand and find answers for problems that we may face in the present.

When we learn about history, we learn about how we have become a nation of Trinibagonians and what it means to us and our country.

Workers at a coffee plantation in Port-of-Spain, Trinidad, in about 1890.

Past, present and future 〉〉〉

When we talk about history, we are really talking about time – the **past**, the **present** and the **future**. When we talk about the past we are talking about the history of a person or a place, or events that happened before the present time. The present is what is happening now and the future is what might or will happen in a time that is still to come.

A **century** is a period of 100 years. We are currently living in the 21st century. A **decade** is a period of 10 years. So, for example, the year 2000 was the first year of the first decade of the 21st century. The year 2010 was the first year of the second decade, and so on.

A **generation** is the time that it takes for children to grow up, become adults and start their own families. A generation is usually considered to be between 25 and 30 years. People of the same generation are people who grow up at around the same time.

Research

Create a large poster or collage showing photographs, charts and maps of Trinidad and Tobago of times past.

Exercise

1. In which century did each of these events occur?

    a) 1976 Trinidad and Tobago becomes a Republic

    b) 1838 Enslaved people emancipated in Trinidad and Tobago

    c) 1962 Dr Eric Williams becomes the first Prime Minister of Trinidad and Tobago

2. In your own words define: past, present, future, century, decade and generation.

We need to know what we can learn from the past and what we need to cherish from the past. We need to know what is special about our nation and ourselves. Here are some ideas about why history is valuable in our lives:

- History helps us to understand who we are. It is part of our identity or collective memory.
- History encourages us to express our own points of view on matters of personal, family and national concern.
- History is interesting and helps to explain why things have happened: why there are so many people of African, East Indian and Chinese ancestry in Trinidad and Tobago.
- History teaches us that we need to respect our cultural heritage.
- History teaches us to reflect on events and lives. Why, for example, were Eric Williams and T.U.B. Butler respected as leaders of our country?
- History teaches us to look at both sides of a problem – there are always two sides to a story. This is a useful skill to apply when we face practical problems in our everyday lives.

Project

Make a timeline of important dates in the history of Trinidad and Tobago. Your teacher will help you to find sources. Here are some to get you started:

- 1498, The Spanish, led by Christopher Columbus, land in Trinidad.
- 1797, The British capture the island of Trinidad.
- 1889, Trinidad and Tobago become one colony.
- 1958, Trinidad and Tobago joins the West Indian Federation.
- 1804, Tobago becomes a British colony.
- 1945, All citizens are given the vote.

When you have done your timeline, discuss the value and relevance of these events in your own life today.

Exercise

3. Define 'history' in your own words.
4. Give three reasons why history is important in our personal lives.
5. What else do you learn about in history besides dates and names?

Discussion

Work in groups, or as a class, with your teacher and discuss the value and relevance of history, and why history is important in your lives today.

Key vocabulary

past

present

future

century

decade

generation

How we study history

We are learning to:
- identify primary and secondary sources
- tell the difference between primary and secondary sources.

History is the study of the past. We learn about history from written texts and other documents called **sources**. We also learn from **oral sources** when people recount their experiences.

Primary sources

A **primary source** is a document or physical object that was written or created at the time. It provides direct or first-hand evidence about an event, object, person or work of art.

Primary sources are usually found in museums and libraries. Examples of primary sources include:

- autobiographies, memoirs, literature, works of art and music
- artefacts (coins, clothing, tools, furniture, fossils)
- photographs, drawings and posters
- audio recordings
- oral sources (interviews with persons who have had first-hand knowledge of an event)
- DVD and video recordings
- diaries, letters, newspaper articles, emails, the internet
- official documents (birth certificates, wills)
- government documents (reports, bills, proclamations, hearings, etc.), research data and reports.

A documentary film or photograph of an event can be a primary source.

Objects that people use, such as clothes, pots, ships and swords, are primary sources.

If you want to find out what life was like in the past, you can study the clothes people wore and the types of transport that they used.

This painting, showing sailing ships in Port-of-Spain in 1860, is an example of a primary source. It helps us to understand that Port-of-Spain was an important harbour at that time.

Exercise

1. Write your own definition of 'primary source' to make sure you understand what it means.

2. How many examples of a primary source can you find in your school?

Activity

Write a short journal entry. Choose any time in the past that you think has significance in your life today. Write about something you did on one day or something that happened in your country on that day.

Secondary sources ▶▶▶

A **secondary source** is a book or document that provides information that was compiled after an event took place. It describes, discusses, interprets, comments upon, analyses, evaluates, summarises and processes primary sources. Secondary sources usually interpret and analyse events that took place in the past. They also add to information from primary sources. Examples of secondary sources include:

- textbooks, bibliographies and biographical works
- reference books such as dictionaries, encyclopaedias and atlases
- articles from journals, magazines and newspapers
- books published after events have occurred
- history books.

Books, such as textbooks or dictionaries, are examples of a secondary source of information.

Bibliographies ▶▶▶

A **bibliography** is a list of the sources (usually secondary sources) that you consult when you are doing research. It is important to show the reader where you have used someone else's ideas or words. The sources are written in alphabetical order according to the surname of the person who wrote the book.

You give the title of the book as well as the name of the publisher and the date when the book was published. For example:

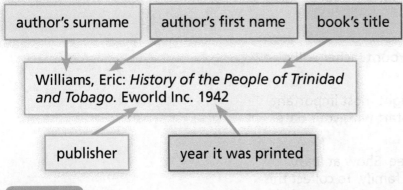

author's surname   author's first name   book's title

Williams, Eric: *History of the People of Trinidad and Tobago*. Eworld Inc. 1942

publisher   year it was printed

Activity

Using the example given as a guide, chose one of your favourite books and write out its details as if you are putting it into a bibliography.

Exercise

3. Write your own definition of 'secondary source' to make sure you understand what it means.

4. How many examples of a secondary source can you find in your school?

5. Who wrote *History of the People of Trinidad and Tobago*? Who published the book? When was it written?

Key vocabulary

source

oral source

primary source

secondary source

bibliography

My personal history

We are learning to:

- trace the history of our families using primary and secondary sources
- do interviews and make observations to collect information about our early lives.

Finding out about my history

There are several things that you can do to trace or find out more about your own life and family history. You can look at primary sources first.

- Look for original documents – birth and death certificates or family photographs.
- One of your ancestors may have written a diary about their experiences.
- You can interview older members of your family, perhaps your grandparents.

Then you can consult secondary sources.

- Find novels and stories written about the times when your parents or grandparents were young.
- Perhaps someone in your family has written an article or a brochure about your family.
- You could also study your family tree if you have one, or you can create your own family tree.

A good place to look for secondary sources is your local library or the school library.

Research project

This project has several parts. Your teacher will give you further guidelines.

1. Create a timeline of the eight most important events in your life so far. Start with your date and place of birth.

2. Create your own family tree. Show at least three generations of your family. To collect this information you can interview members of your family and you can use primary sources like birth, marriage and death certificates.

3. Collect photographs of your family if you can and make a poster of your family tree. Use this poster to make a presentation to the rest of the class. Explain the **kinship** between the family members and explain how you collected your information.

> **Did you know...?**
>
> Your **next of kin** are the members of your immediate family – your mother, father, brothers and sisters.

Your **personal history** is the history of the people from whom you are descended (your ancestors) and the people to whom you are related.

What do you know about your personal history?

- **Place of birth** – Where were you born? Were your parents and grandparents born in the same place?
- **Ancestral lineage** – Who were your grandparents and your great-great grandparents?
- **Kinship** – Do you know all of the people who are related to you by descent, not marriage?
- **Religion** – Do you and all members of your family follow a religion? If so, do you all follow the same religion?
- **Customs** – Where do your family customs come from?
- **Documents** – What information do family birth certificates or marriage certificates provide?
- **Family tree** – A diagram that shows the generations of a family and how they are related to each other.

My full name is _____

I am _____ years old. I was born on

_____

I was born in _____ area

I am now _____ tall (centimetres)

I weigh _____ (kilos)

My parents/guardian are _____

My religion is _____

Two family customs are: (1) _____

(2) _____

My favourite sport is _____

I live at _____

(Insert your fingerprint or photograph or a drawing of yourself here)

Exercise

1. Give an example of two documents that are primary sources of information.
2. What could you create to show your kinship relations?
3. Name two items of information that you could include in your personal history.
4. Compile a personal history form (see the example above).

Key vocabulary

kinship

next of kin

personal history

place of birth

ancestral lineage

religion

customs

documents

family tree

Comparing lives

We are learning to:

- compare and contrast our lives with the lives of our parents and grandparents
- appreciate that we are part of a community and that we share goals and principles.

> **Comparing and contrasting lives** 》

Life can change a lot from one generation to the next. New people with different cultures might come to live in the **community** and there may be other changes as a result of technology or perhaps political events.

Think about your grandparents, for example, and the ways in which your experiences are different from or similar to their experiences.

- *Where were your grandparents born?* Were they born in Trinidad and Tobago? If not, where were they born? Can you find that place on a map? Is that country very different from Trinidad and Tobago or, are there similarities?
- *What clothes did they wear?* The clothes were probably very different from the clothes that you wear. The women in those days probably only wore long dresses, for example.
- *How did they travel around?* Did your grandparents have cars? Did they use carriages or ox wagons? Did they have to walk to school? Today we usually go to school by bus or car. People in past generations often walked as far as 20 km a day to get to school and back again.
- *What about your religion?* Perhaps you follow the same religion as your grandparents. You may therefore have a very similar religious experience to that of your grandparents.
- *Do you have family traditions?* Some families have special traditions, such as eating special meals at special times or following certain careers or sporting activities. Where do these traditions come from? Have these traditions changed as times have changed?

> **Project**

Compile a table similar to this one with areas to compare and contrast. You can discuss and add ideas of your own. Other areas to compare could be games played, dress, manners, communication, transport or technology.

Areas to compare and contrast	Grandparents	Parents	Children today
Work expected to do as children			
Rights of women			
Religious practices			
Festivals enjoyed			
Stories enjoyed			

Most communities in Trinidad and Tobago are diverse because people from many different cultures and ancestries live and work there. Families in communities may share **principles**, goals and **traditions** despite coming from different cultural backgrounds. For example, people may share the principle of respecting elders, they may share a goal like wanting their children to get a good education and they may all enjoy and share a traditional festival or carnival.

In peaceful communities people work together despite their differences. People respect and accept their differences. We learn about each other's values, customs, religions and foods. We share our knowledge and exchange ideas. Our communities are richer and stronger because of this diversity.

This is a picture of Duke Street and Piccadilly Hill in Port-of-Spain, Trinidad, March 1927. Can you find a picture of what it looks like today?

Research

Working in groups, create a brochure of information about the beliefs, customs, ceremonies and traditions of different families in your community.

a) Compare these beliefs and say how they are similar or different.

b) Use primary and secondary sources to collect information.

c) Include a bibliography with your brochure to show which sources you have consulted.

d) Draw up a timeline of events in your community. Your teacher will help you to decide in what year the timeline should start.

e) Present your work to the rest of the class.

Discussion

As a class, discuss the changes that have taken place in your community in the last two generations. To prepare for this discussion, interview some older members of your community and look for photographs and documents with relevant information.

Exercise

1. Write down two suggestions about how people can live together peacefully in a community despite having different ancestry.

2. Give an example of a tradition that you share with other members of your class.

3. Give an example of a principle that you share with other members of your community.

Project

Imagine that you went to school 100 years ago. Write a journal entry about a day in your life.

a) Would you have walked to school?

b) What clothes would you have worn?

c) How would you have done your homework?

d) What would you have done in the afternoon and evening?

Key vocabulary

community

principles

traditions

The history of my school

We are learning to:

- trace the history of our sources
- collect information through interviews and observations
- work collaboratively to produce a history of our school.

Tracing the history of my school ❯❯

Some schools in Trinidad and Tobago have long, proud traditions. Your own school may be new or it may have started years ago. The people who started the school will have set out their **vision** for it and considered questions like these:

- What type of school is it and who will attend?
- What will be taught at the school (the **curriculum**)?
- Will the students wear a **uniform** and what will that be? How many students will be admitted?
- Where will the lessons take place? Who will teach the students?
- Will there be **extra-curricular** and sports activities?
- Who will lead the school?

Case study

The Far Hills High School is a landmark in the community. The school was **established** in 1953 and its **rationale** was to empower boys and girls of all religions and races to achieve academic success. The school provided education for children who lived in the area, who had previously had to travel far to attend school.

The school opened with 43 students in four classrooms. The school offered a full academic programme as well as extra-curricular activities such as sports, music and drama. Students from the school have distinguished themselves in many walks of life.

Over the years the school has grown. New classrooms have been added and there are now 450 students.

Questions

1. Why was the Far Hills School set up?
2. Do you think all children in the community were welcomed at this school?
3. Has the Far Hills School been successful in serving its community? Explain your answer.

Activity

Working in pairs, study the photograph of the old school classroom on page 17. Compare this classroom with your own classroom.

Discussion

What do you know about the history of your own school? Discuss the history of your school with your teacher.

When researching the history of your school, you will need to think about:

- why it was set up and when
- the vision, **mission** and extra-curricular activities
- uniforms, buildings, sports and awards
- the legacy of the school, principal, teachers, students
- customs and traditions of the school.

There are many different ways of finding out about the history of your own school. You can start by observing your school buildings and sources of information at your school. Your school library may have information like this:

- Primary sources such as photographs that show the school at different times
- Copies of old school magazines with photographs and articles about school life during a specific year
- Trophies and honour rolls that record the achievements of students over the years.

Older members of the community can provide interesting information about daily life at school. You can set up interviews with some people. Draw up a questionnaire with questions similar to these:

- Did you attend this school?
- Which subjects did you study?
- Did you do any extra-curricular activities?
- Were you punished if you did not obey rules? How?
- What were your best memories of the school?

Secondary sources such as articles in magazines and newspapers can also provide valuable information about schools. You can search the websites of local newspapers for articles.

> **Did you know...?**
>
> In 1825 there were only six schools on the island of Trinidad. One was an English female boarding school, three were French day schools in Port-of-Spain, one school was maintained by the Cabildo for teaching the English language, and a small day school was being operated in an Amerindian village where only Spanish was taught.

Project

Working in groups, and then as a class, produce a booklet about the history of your school. To do this you will need to do some careful planning and then work cooperatively. Everyone in the class should make a contribution.

The information that you collect should come from interviews and other primary and secondary sources. You should also compile a bibliography to acknowledge the sources you have used and create a timeline to show the major events in the school's history.

> **Key vocabulary**
>
> **vision**
>
> **curriculum (curricula)**
>
> **uniform**
>
> **extra-curricular**
>
> **established**
>
> **rationale**
>
> **mission**

The role and legacy of my school

We are learning to:

- compare our school lives with the school lives from different times and places in our country
- appreciate the role and legacy of my school.

School life at different times ⟩⟩

Over the years, schools have changed. For example:

- The government has developed new curricula to guide teachers about what should be taught in class.
- Some schools have changed their school uniforms.
- Many schools have improved their structures and built new classrooms, science laboratories, libraries and sports facilities.
- New technology has been brought into classrooms. Teachers and students now use computers, tablets and interactive light boards instead of chalkboards and slates.
- As students, you are encouraged to take a more active role in learning, so there is more discussion and research.
- All children, boys and girls, have access to free education in Trinidad and Tobago.

In the past, not everyone had access to schools and education was not compulsory. Children from poor families were often not able to go to school because they had to help their parents at home, and the parents could not afford to pay for school fees and uniforms. More boys received an education than girls.

The mission of the Trinidad and Tobago Ministry of Education in 2015 is to educate and develop children who are:

- able to fulfil their full potential
- healthy and growing normally
- academically balanced
- well-adjusted socially and culturally
- emotionally mature and happy.

Exercise

1. In what ways has technology changed how we learn at school?
2. How have classrooms changed in schools over the years? Think about what you use in your classroom to learn.
3. Why do you think the curriculum has changed in the last 50 years? Give an example of a subject in which you learn different content from what your parents learned, for example.
4. Do you think that you receive a good education at your school? How could your education be improved?

Discussion

Discuss what it meant to children who did not have free access to good education in the past. What happened to them? What work did they do?

Activity

Write a journal entry in which you reflect on what you have learned about your school and the role your school plays in your community.

The role of your school ▶▶▶

Your school helps to educate students such as yourself in your community. It also provides a place where students and their families interact and get to know each other.

The principal, teachers, parents and students at the school all have a role to play. For example, the principal will provide guidance and vision, the teachers will facilitate and provide good learning experiences for the students, the parents will support and encourage the school and the students will study and learn.

Working together **cooperatively** helps to ensure a good education for the students.

The legacy of your school ▶▶▶

Each generation of teachers and students builds up a **legacy**, which will benefit students in the future. A legacy of academic or sporting success will inspire future generations of students. Students will want to follow in the footsteps of others at the school who have succeeded.

Good academic achievements will help you to get a place in a good university when you leave school. Playing in the first cricket team at your school may help you on the path to a professional career in cricket.

Sports stars such as Ato Boldon and Brian Lara, singer Billy Ocean, writer V.S. Naipaul, politician Eric Williams, and many others, have all inspired future generations.

Ex-students can become role models for current students, or donate their time, expertise and money to improve conditions at the school.

1.6

Principal:
responsible for managing the major administrative tasks and supervising all students and teachers

⬇

Vice Principal:
works alongside school principals to manage the administrative and educational components of a school

⬇

Heads of Department (HOD):
responsible for the running of their department (e.g. science, languages)

⬇

Teachers:
work alongside the HODs to provide a good learning environment and experience for students to learn in

⬇

Students:
will study and learn

Exercise

5. In your own words describe the different roles and responsibilities that people have at school.

6. Read the mission statement of the Ministry of Education. In your own words, describe what each point means.

7. Why do you think your school is an important part of your community?

Brian Lara is an inspiration for children to take up cricket.

The role and legacy of students »

A legacy is something tangible or intangible that is passed on from one generation to another. A school's legacy, for example, could be something physical, such as the architecture, books and equipment used by generations of students. Alternatively, it could be something intangible, such as a work ethos or a commitment to supporting the local community. Legacies are important as they shape a school's identity and, ultimately, impacts on your individual identity. More importantly, legacies immortalize schools.

A school's legacy is molded by everyone in the institution – the students, principal, teachers, office staff and the janitors. Legacies help us form connections with the past and act as instruments of motivation and inspiration to others.

Case study

Queen's Royal College (QRC) is one of the oldest all-male government secondary schools in Trinidad and Tobago. The school has produced several famous persons, including:

Queen's Royal College (QRC), Port of Spain.

- Dr Eric Williams, the country's first Prime Minister. He was an outstanding student at QRC, matched by his achievements on the football field. At Oxford University in England, he obtained a B.A. in History and Political Science in 1935 and a Doctorate in Philosophy in 1938. His thesis, *Economic Aspects of the Abolition of the West Indian Slave Trade and Slavery*, gave an indication of the direction he would follow.

  In 1939, he joined the faculty of social and political science at Howard University, and also became associated with the Caribbean Commission, which coordinated the economic development of the Caribbean area. In 1956, he founded the People's National Movement, eventually leading Trinidad and Tobago to independence in 1962. He subsequently became the country's first and longest serving prime minister between 1962 and his death in 1981.

Carnival and costume designer Peter Minshall at home in Trinidad.

- Peter Minshall was born in Guyana in 1941 but grew up in Trinidad, where he attended QRC, becoming involved in the school's theatrical performances. He obtained a Diploma at the Central School of Art and Design in London and designed his first major work, *Land of the Hummingbird*. He went on to be heavily involved in the opening ceremonies of both the 1994 Soccer World Cup in Chicago, and also the 1992 Barcelona Olympic Games.

- Richard Thompson won silver medal in the 2008 Olympic 100m in Beijing, and gold in

Richard Thompson at the Beijing Olympic Games 2008.

the 4 × 100m relay. He was also a member of the relay team that won silver at the 2012 London Olympics.

- Cyril Lionel Robert (C.L.R) James (1901–89) was a keen sportsman while at QRC. He graduated in 1918, returning to teach English and History – one of his students being a young Eric Williams. He moved to England to help write the biography of the West Indian cricketer Learie Constantine. His *Beyond the Boundary* in 1963 is often cited as being the best book ever written about cricket. He was the first black West Indian to have a book published in Britain – *Mint Alley* in 1936. His notable works as a political activist include *World Revolution* (1937) and *Haitian Revolution: The Black Jacobins* (1938).

- Other alumni include Derryck Murray, West Indian wicket keeper 1963–80; Darcus Howe, broadcaster; Wendell Mottley, 1964 Olympic silver medallist and politician; George Maxwell Richards, first President of Trinidad and Tobago 2003–13.

This school's legacy is linked to its:

- Motto – *Certant Omnes Sed Non Omnibus Palma* – It is the effort that really counts even though only one may win the prize
- Vision – Excellence in Education
- Mission – To so educate our students in a creative and dynamic learning environment that they will achieve their full potential academically, emotionally, physically, socially and spiritually.

QRC's legacy not only inspires students to produce their best and make an impact in society, it also connects them to the historical development of Trinidad and Tobago.

Activity

1. Write a journal entry on how your school's legacy has impacted your life thus far.

2. Speak to staff, and if possible alumni, to gather their thoughts on what the school's legacy is, and compare it to what you and your peers think it is.

3. Identify a teacher from your school and discuss his/her legacy.

Discussion

Group work: In groups of 6 or 8 hold the following discussion: "Time changes everything, do you agree?" Can the legacy of principals, teachers and students change over time? Discuss. Each group share their findings with the class

Exercise

9. What is your school's motto? What does it mean?

10. Research a famous person from Trinidad and Tobago. Find out what school they attended, the motto of that school, and link the achievements of the famous individual to the concepts in the school's motto.

11. How do you think your teachers or principal have nurtured and preserved your school's legacy?

12. Do you think a school's legacy can change over time? What elements do you think are responsible for this change?

Key vocabulary

cooperatively

legacy

The life of Lord Harris

We are learning to:

- examine the life, contribution and legacy of Lord Harris
- explain how the present is connected to the past.

The contribution of Lord Harris

Lord Harris was the governor of Trinidad from 1846 to 1851 and from 1852 to 1854. He is considered to be the best governor ever to come to Trinidad because of the way he improved our systems of politics, communications and education.

Politics

Lord Harris arrived at a time when Trinidad was starting to develop. Enslaved people had been emancipated and Indian **indentured** labourers had started arriving to work on the plantations.

His government helped the new **immigrants** to settle in Trinidad, but he also realised that certain reforms were necessary if the freed people and the new arrivals were to become part of the society on the island. He declared that "a race has been freed, but a society has not been formed [on Trinidad]".

His first step was to divide the island into counties and wards (districts) in order to provide better services from the government. Then he set about providing other services, such as water supplies. He started a project to lay down water pipes in Port-of-Spain.

The first public library in Trinidad was set up in this building by Lord Harris. Today, the 'Red House' is the seat of government of Trinidad and Tobago.

Communications

Lord Harris started the first public library in Trindad and Tobago, in Port-of-Spain. He also set up the first inland postal service. This allowed people in San Fernando to send letters by post to people in Port-of-Spain. Towards the end of his term of office, a steamer boat was named after him in honour of his achievements.

Project

Working as a group, create a timeline of the life and achievements of Lord Harris. Use any primary and secondary sources you can find. Then present your report to the class.

Exercise

1. Who was Lord Harris?
2. During which periods was he in Trinidad?

The education system that we have today is partly a result of the changes that Lord Harris introduced during his term of office (in the past).

The Roman Catholic Church and some other organisations set up the first schools in Trinidad during the time when the Spanish ruled the island. The British started a formal education system when they arrived. But by 1825 there were only six schools on the island, as we discovered in unit 1.5.

Lord Harris believed that, because of the diversity of religious beliefs and cultural backgrounds, education should be provided by the government. He also believed that education should be **secular**; in other words, not connected to any specific religious instruction. He wrote in 1851:

> I am desirous that the means and the opportunities for obtaining instructions should be afforded to every child in this island.

In 1846 his government passed a law which authorised a new school system called the Ward School System. Under this system 30 **ward schools** were set up. The law required that one **public** (government) **school** should be set up in each ward (district) of the island. The students who attended these schools did not pay school fees and no religious instruction was allowed.

A board of education was created to supervise the schools and an inspector was appointed to check on activities in the schools. A school for training teachers was also set up in Port-of-Spain. So, for the first time in the history of the island, the children of enslaved people who had been emancipated, and indentured labourers were able to attend free public schools.

This drama class in Black Rock Tobago Secondary School is partly due to the work of Lord Harris in the 19th century.

Discussion

Have a class discussion about the contribution of Lord Harris to the development of Trinidad and Tobago as a nation. What do you think was the most important part of his contribution? Why?

Exercise

3. What problems did Lord Harris identify when he came to Trinidad?
4. Explain briefly what a ward school was.
5. How did Lord Harris contribute to the political development of Trinidad?
6. What did Lord Harris do to improve communications on the island?
7. Explain how you think the schools of today are linked to the work done by Lord Harris.

Key vocabulary
....

indentured

immigrants

secular

ward school

public school

The past and the present

We are learning to:

- identify similarities and differences between the past and the present
- appreciate how people lived in earlier times and how their lives would be different today.

Similarities and differences between the past and the present

There are **similarities** and **differences** between life on Trinidad and Tobago in the past and life today. Let us look at a few examples.

Government

Think about the type of government that we have. Today's government is **democratically** elected. All adults older than age 18 can vote for who will represent us there. During the time of Lord Harris only a few citizens were able to vote and the governor was appointed by the British monarchy. Most people then had very little say in how they were governed, whereas today people have a lot more say.

Agricultural workers splitting coconuts during harvest time in Tobago, 1934.

Community life

Some aspects of community life have remained the same. For example, people still celebrate their **traditional** customs during festivals and everyone is encouraged to join in. People are also able to vote in local government elections and choose their own leaders to attend to issues that concern their communities. Many people have moved from their traditional communities to urban areas to look for jobs. Their way of life changes when they move.

Transport and travel

People arrived in Trinidad and Tobago on ships that took months to arrive. Nowadays, if someone wants to go and visit family and relatives elsewhere in the world they can do so by catching a flight. Cars, buses and aeroplanes provide the main means of transportation today. Ox-wagons, horses and carriages are no longer used. Modern transport is much faster and more efficient than older forms of transport.

Activity

Create a display in your school on the topic of the 'past and present'.

Case study

Farming – past and present

Farming in the northern hills of Trinidad has been going on for years, but it has changed a lot. One farmer from Maracas Bay, whose family has lived and farmed there for more than three generations, remembers some of the changes that have occurred.

"In my father's time farmers used very few chemicals on their crops. They did not use **fertilisers** and they only used pesticides when there were infestations of insects like mole crickets for example."

Today, farmers rely on chemical fertilisers and pesticides to produce bigger crops, but there is a feeling that crops may no longer be safe to eat as a result.

So now farmers are turning back to more environmentally friendly farming methods.

They prefer to use natural composts to strengthen and improve the soil as a way of producing better crops.

Questions

1. Think about Trinidad and Tobago in the 19th century and compare those times with your life today. Give examples of:

    a) a difference in the way Trinidad and Tobago was governed

    b) a difference in the way people travelled

    c) a similarity in the way farmers worked

    d) a difference in the education system

    e) a similarity in community life.

2. Do you think life is generally better today than it was in the time of your grandparents? Explain your answer and give examples.

3. Pretend that you are a farmer 75 years ago. Write a journal entry about how you dealt with your crops today.

4. Look for pictures or draw pictures that illustrate the differences between now and then.

Project

Digital storytelling is a short form of digital media production that allows everyday people to share aspects of their life story. People are filmed as they tell their life stories. These films can provide a lot of insight into the lives of people.

Your teacher will play you a story like this, which you can discuss. Work in groups and make your own digital story about yourselves. You can also include members of your family or community. Take turns to describe interesting parts of your lives on the recording. Play your recordings for others in the class.

Case study

Community Life in 1962

The year is 1962. Samuel's mother sent him to the shop to purchase some soft drinks in order to celebrate Trinidad and Tobago's independence. Samuel went to the shop and got the items on 'trust' from Mr Chin the owner.

On his walk back he made a mental note to write a letter to his pen pal from London tonight, so that he can post it the following day. He hailed some of his friends who were playing hop scotch, pitch and rescue catch on the street.

Samuel took a deep breath as he savoured the aroma of Ms Pat's cooking and waved to her as he passed in front of her outdoor kitchen.

Samuel quickened his pace as he realised it was getting late and did not want to miss papa's storytelling time. Every evening his papa would tell stories to all the grandchildren who dutifully came and listened with great delight. He returned just in time to hear his papa's stories.

Questions

1. What is meant by the term 'trust'? What does this tell us about Samuel's community?

2. List three differences and three similarities between Samuel's life and community and present-day life and community.

3. Chat with your grandparents and parents to find out other differences between their community life and present-day community life.

Exercise

1. **a)** Is the art if story telling alive today?

   b) If so, how is it being preserved?

2. **a)** Are there any differences in the way stories are told today than in the past?

   b) If so, what are the differences?

3. How has this art been preserved?

Activity

Write a short journal entry on your likes and dislikes of community life in the 1960s and the present day, giving reasons for them.

Discussion

Group work: In groups of six or eight, hold the following discussion: "Time can either kill or give new life to old traditions". Do you agree? Discuss. Each group share their findings with the class.

Key vocabulary

similarities

differences

democratically

traditional

fertilisers

digital storytelling

Questions

See how well you have understood the topics in this unit.

1. A decade is a period of _____ years.

   a) 1000   **b)** 20

   c) 10   **d)** 50

2. A period of 100 years is called a _____ .

   a) century   **b)** centenary

   c) millennium   **d)** generation

3. Which of these is not a primary source of information?

   a) a diary

   b) a photograph

   c) a textbook

   d) a news report about a current event

4. Which of these is a secondary source?

   a) a birth certificate

   b) a dictionary

   c) a radio interview

   d) an artefact

5. True or false? Your grandparents are part of your ancestral lineage.

6. Fill in the blanks of what a bibliography shows.

   Williams, Eric: *History of the People of Trinidad and Tobago.* Eworld Inc. 1942

7. Complete the sentence: A secular education does not include _____ education.

8. The achievements that are handed down to future generations are referred to as a _____ .

   a) legal

   b) legacy

   c) lineage

   d) generation

9. A _____ is a list of sources you have consulted, arranged in alphabetical order.

   a) bible

   b) secondary

   c) bibliography

   d) biography

10. Correct these statements:

   a) 1789 is a date in the 17th century.

   b) Lord Harris served as governor of Trinidad for more than a generation, from 1846 to 1854.

   c) Mathematics is a subject in the school calendar.

11. Complete the timeline information below:

   _____ The Spanish, led by Christopher Columbus, land in Trinidad.

   1797, The British capture the island of _____ .

   1889, Trinidad and Tobago become one colony, _____ .

   1958, _____ joins the West Indian Federation.

   1804, _____ becomes a British Colony.

   _____ , all citizens are given the vote.

12. Explain what Lord Harris meant when he said "a race has been freed, but a society has not been formed".

13. Explain how you can take an active role in your own education.

14. How have schools in Trinidad and Tobago changed in the last 50 years? Give two examples.

15. Lord Harris believed that, in order for Trinidad to develop, certain changes had to occur in education. Which of these statements summarises these changes?

   a) All students had to be taught in English.

   b) All children in Trinidad had to have an education that was free and secular.

   c) All children had to receive free religious education.

   d) All children were obliged to attend ward schools.

16. Explain what the difference is between a primary source and a secondary source.

17. Name two important contributions that Lord Harris made to the development of communication in Trinidad and say why you think each was important.

18. Give two reasons why you feel history is important in your life. Explain your answer.

19. Explain how and why you should work cooperatively at school.

20. Write a journal entry in which you imagine that you lived at a time in the past. Describe a day in your life. Give your journal a date.

21. Explain the roles and responsibilities of the principal, the parents, the students and the teachers at your school.

22. Give two examples of areas of our lives in which we can see how the present is connected to the past.

23. Make a table in which you give three examples each of primary and secondary sources.

24. "A people without the knowledge of their past history, origin and culture is like a tree without roots." Explain what this means giving examples from your personal history.

25. What is a pen pal?

26. Do you still use letters to communicate with friends today? If not, what do you use to communicate?

27. Do you play hopscotch, pitch and rescue catch with your friends? If not, what games do you play?

28. Find out how the game of pitch is played. Try a game in your school yard.

29. What do you understand by the word legacy?

30. What do you think is your school's legacy?

31. How can you contribute to your school's legacy now and in the future?

Checking your progress

To make good progress in understanding the value and relevance of history/the past, check that you understand these ideas.

Explain in your own words the value and relevance of history.

Explain what a primary and a secondary source are.

Give three examples of a primary and a secondary source.

Name four sources where you can find out about your family's history.

Name four types of information that you should include in your personal history.

Explain why it is important that we appreciate that we are part of a larger community.

Name four types of information that you should include when considering tracing the history of your school.

Name four ways that schools have changed today from times past.

Explain why it is important that we appreciate the role and legacy of our school in our community.

Explain the contribution made by Lord Harris to education in Trinidad and Tobago.

Explain the development of the education system in Trinidad and Tobago under Lord Harris.

Describe the similarities and differences in two areas of life in Trinidad and Tobago between the past and today.

Unit 2: My community

My community

- The path to colonialism, life as a Crown Colony
- The transatlantic slave trade, emancipation
- Immigration and indentureship, migration and peasant farming
- Diversification and the unification of Trinidad and Tobago

Sources of historical data

- Primary sources

Historical sites and landmarks

- Describe historical sites and landmarks in the community
- The origins and significance of historical sites and landmarks
- Evaluate multiple sources of information

Social composition of the community

- Historical factors that have contributed to the social development of the community
- The impact of historical events such as
  - slavery, indentureship, inter-island migration
- the social development of various communities:
  - gender, race, class
- Value the diversity of various communities

Economic development of the community

- The historical factors that have contributed to the economic development of the community
- Development of industries, such as sugar, cocoa, oil, rice
- Compare the economic development of various communities
  - life in the village and the city

The path to colonialism

We are learning to:

- define and apply various concepts: colonialism and Crown Colony.

Colonialism　》

Colonialism is when a powerful country, such as Britain, directly controls less powerful countries, such as Trinidad, and uses that country's resources to increase its own power and wealth.

The path to colonialism　》》

We have seen how Trinidad was a Spanish colony until 1797, how the French captured Trinidad in 1781 and how from 1797 Trinidad became subjected to British rule.

Tobago was also subjected to European control by the Dutch and British in the 17th century, the French from 1781 and then back to the British from 1803. In 1783, the Spanish king issued the Cedula of Population. This law granted free land to Roman Catholics from other Caribbean islands that were willing to settle in Trinidad.

Many French settlers **migrated** to Trinidad and brought **enslaved** Africans with them. This led to the expansion of the cocoa and sugar plantations.

After Britain gained control of Trinidad in 1797, the British began to **exploit** the natural resources of Trinidad. Raw materials, such as sugar, were exported back to Britain to be refined, and Trinidad became more reliant on imported goods.

To maximise the opportunity for wealth, the British brought in large numbers of enslaved African people to work on the plantations. The enslaved Africans were subjected to terrible conditions on their journey. Many died making the crossing from Africa.

Project

Throughout this unit you will create a timeline of events. Start with creating a timeline of events in Trinidad, from the time of the arrival of the Spanish to when Tobago was annexed to Trinidad in 1889. Add short notes about the importance of the dates.

Exercise

1. In your own words, define colonialism.
2. What was the Cedula of Population?
3. Following the Cedula of Population, which settlers migrated to Trinidad?
4. How did the British exploit Trinidad and Tobago for commercial gain?

Did you know...?

Before it was unified with Trinidad in 1789, Tobago was colonised by the European colonial powers of France, Holland and Britain 22 times in total.

From about 1880, income from plantations began to drop and the cost of governing Trinidad (and later Tobago) became too expensive for the British Government. Soon, British Government colonialism began to cause greater social, economic and political unrest.

Life as a Crown Colony

When the British arrived, Spanish laws remained for a few years. However, in 1802 Trinidad was officially made a British **Crown Colony**. The ruling system was made up of:

- a Governor, who ruled the island and represented the British Crown in London
- a Legislative Council, chosen by the Governor to help him run the island.

When the British first arrived, the British Crown allowed the Cabildo, which represented the taxpayers on the island, to advise the Governor. These taxpayers were mostly plantation owners. However, the Cabildo favoured policies that the British Crown did not always prefer, so the system was changed to one in which the Governor appointed a Legislative Council, which advised and assisted in the governing of the colony.

Sir Arthur Hamilton-Gordon Governor of Trinidad, 1866–70.

The people on Trinidad were now subject to British law. The Crown also retained the right to **override** any decisions made in the colony that they thought were unsuitable. As we have seen, the British played a part in the development of Trinidad.

- As the sugar cane industry began to develop, transportation systems needed to be introduced to enable the plantations to export their crops.
- Wholesale and retail businesses were set up as a direct result of the sugar cane industry.
- The education system was improved.

Tobago became a British Crown Colony in 1876 and remained so until its annexation to Trinidad in 1889.

Exercise

5. In which year was Trinidad officially made a Crown Colony?

6. In your own words, explain the Crown Colony system introduced by the British to Trinidad.

7. Who were the Cabildo?

8. Did the British make any contribution to the development of Trinidad and Tobago?

9. Do you think colonialism was good or bad for the islands? Write 100–150 words.

Key vocabulary

colonialism

migrated

enslaved

exploit

Crown Colony

override

The transatlantic slave trade

We are learning to:

- define and apply various concepts: transatlantic slave trade and emancipation.

Africans come to Trinidad »

The **transatlantic slave trade** was the forced movement of people from Africa to the American continent in the 18th century, to be sold and enslaved. In this period, most of the African people who moved to Trinidad and Tobago were enslaved and brought to the islands to provide labour for the sugar plantations.

- 1610 – the Dutch brought 400 enslaved Africans to Trinidad.
- 1783 – the Spanish Cedula of Population saw an increase in enslaved Africans arrive from other Caribbean islands.
- 1783 onwards – the Spanish Cedula of Population saw a further 10 000 enslaved Africans arrive on the island.
- 1797 – the number of enslaved Africans in Trinidad is 10 000.
- 1797 – the arrival of the British saw an expansion in the sugar industry. More enslaved people were brought from Africa to work on the plantations.
- 1802 – the number of enslaved Africans in Trinidad had increased to over 20 000.

The enslaved Africans came from Central and West Africa, in particular the Hausa, Yoruba, Congolese, Igbo and Malinké communities.

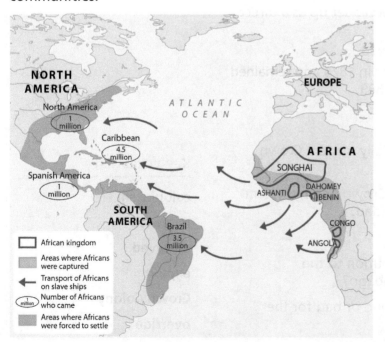

1610: Around 400 enslaved African people arrive

1783: Enslaved people from other Caribbean countries arrive with French settlers

1797: The number of enslaved Africans in Trinidad is 10 000

1802: Number of enslaved Africans increases to around 22 000

Emancipation is the removal of restraint or restrictions on an individual or a group of people. The slave trade was a very profitable business for nearly 300 years. Enslaved people all over the world were treated with great cruelty. They were forced to do hard manual labour and live under terrible conditions. So why did this end? There were humanitarian, intellectual and economic reasons for this.

- Strong moral convictions led people to believe that slavery was an **inhumane** practice.
- People were also becoming more aware of humanitarian ideas like liberty and equality, and the concept that everyone should have these rights, not just a few privileged people.
- Economists argued that slave labour was inefficient, and that the cost of having enslaved people was more expensive than paying for hired help.
- Economists wanted **free trade** policies, which meant buying from the cheapest supplier. Sugar from the plantations where enslaved people were forced to work was more expensive than sugar from other countries, where labourers were paid for the work they did.
- Plantation owners had begun to face competition from the sugar beet industry in European countries.

In Britain, a Member of Parliament called William Wilberforce heard about the terrible conditions under which enslaved people were brought to the West Indies. He introduced a bill in the British Parliament to stop the practice of slavery in the British Empire. He died soon after the law was passed.

On 1 August 1834, the Emancipation Bill came into effect. This **abolished** slavery in the British Empire, including Trinidad. On 1 August 1985, Trinidad and Tobago became the first country in the world to declare a national holiday to commemorate the abolition of slavery. We now celebrate Emancipation Day annually.

William Wilberforce is remembered for his campaigns to stop the trade in enslaved people.

Discussion

Discuss these questions in groups: 'If you had been a plantation owner, would you have supported or opposed the abolition of slavery? Why/why not?'

Exercise

1. Explain in your own words what led to the emancipation of enslaved people.

2. How did the ideas of liberty and equality affect people's attitude to the slave trade?

3. Take dates related to slave trade, slavery and emancipation, then add them to your timeline.

Key vocabulary

transatlantic slave trade

emancipation

inhumane

free trade

abolish

Immigration and indentureship

We are learning to:

- define and apply various concepts: immigration, indentureship, belief systems.

Indentureship

When slavery was abolished in 1838, most of the enslaved people left the plantations to set up their own small farms and industries. This meant that there were not enough people to work on the plantations and this affected the economy of the islands.

The plantation owners approached the British government to set up an **immigration** system to help with the labour shortage. This became known as **indentureship**. The **immigrants** came on a voluntary basis, unlike the earlier enslaved people, who were forced. Indenture was a system where persons gave their labour willingly and were bound by a contract to work for an employer for a fixed term, usually on the plantations. Upon completion of the contract, they were free to go.

European immigrants from Ireland, Germany and Portugal started to arrive in Trinidad from 1839. They were often destitute or homeless, and came to start a new life. From 1806, many Chinese people also came to Trinidad and Tobago.

Most of the immigrants at this time came from India. Between 1845 and 1917, about 144 000 East Indians came to Trinidad and Tobago under the indentured labour system. The indentured system came to an end in 1917.

Some Indian immigrants decided to stay and make Trinidad their permanent home after they had completed their indenture. They brought their families to the islands, bought land and started their own businesses. Today the descendants of these labourers make up 35–40% of the population of Trinidad and Tobago.

1839: First European immigrants arrive

⋁⋁

1845: First Indian labourers arrive aboard the ship *Fatel Razack*

⋁⋁

1853–66: Chinese immigrants arrive

⋁⋁

1917: System of indentured labour comes to an end

Did you know...?

One scheme allowed male Indians who had lived in Trinidad for 10 years to get 10 acres (4 hectares) of Crown land instead of a free return to India.

Exercise

1. In your own words, define **a)** immigration and **b)** indentureship.

2 Write a short explanation of the differences between slavery and indentureship.

3 Explain briefly why indentured labourers came from India to Trinidad and Tobago.

Research

Work in pairs. Find out more about an Indian or Chinese family that came to work in Trinidad. Complete this for homework.

There are many factors that contributed to the end of the system of indenture. For example:

- Nationalism in India – India was a British colony at this time and a **nationalist** movement was taking root. Leaders like Mahatma Gandhi and Gopal Krishna Gokhale questioned the system of indenture.

- Humanitarian ideas – In 1911, the Government of India issued a statement about the indenture system. It said that "more and more [people] were coming to believe that the system is objectionable and should be discontinued".

- Unhappiness about working and living conditions – workers in Trinidad were unhappy with their low wages and the lack of jobs, and some blamed the indenture system for this. The Indian immigrants were also finding work on the plantations less and less attractive. Although the Government put systems in place to protect the immigrant workers, it was not very effective.

- The living conditions of the immigrants were poor, they were not able to move around freely, and many workers were mistreated and punished severely for minor offences. Eventually this led to clashes with the authorities.

- The Indian immigrants started to leave the big plantations to become small independent sugar farmers. By 1902, more than half the sugar produced on Trinidad was produced by these independent farmers.

- Disruptions caused by World War I – from 1914 until 1918, the world was at war. This caused disruptions in shipping, which meant that workers could not travel safely between India and Trinidad and Tobago.

Newly arrived Indians in Trinidad, circa 1897.

Did you know...?

About 2500 Chinese immigrated to Trinidad between 1853 and 1866. After indentureship they became shopkeepers, tradesmen and engaged in market gardening.

Did you know...?

Indian Arrival Day is celebrated on 30 May every year in Trinidad and Tobago – the first country to start this holiday.

Exercise

4. Explain in your own words the factors that contributed to the end of the indentured labour system.

5. Work in pairs. Make a poster that shows the cultural influence of these Indian immigrants on the islands of Trinidad and Tobago. Think about food, music, names and businesses.

6. Take key dates from the information you have studied and add them to your timeline.

Key vocabulary

immigration

indentured/indentureship

immigrant

nationalist

Peasant farming

We are learning to:

• define and apply various concepts: peasantry and migration.

Farming after emancipation – peasant farming ⟩⟩

In the aftermath of emancipation, there was **migration** of people within Trinidad and Tobago. This was caused by:

• movement of **formerly enslaved people** to set up peasant farms
• movement after indentureship periods had expired

Peasant farmers acquired post-emancipation land through:

• being allowed to stay on estate land
• saving money, or pooling resources to buy land
• renting small areas of land
• squatting on land owned by the Crown.

This was the beginning of **peasant farming** in Trinidad and Tobago, which is basic small-scale farming for subsistence, with any surplus being sold in local markets. Peasant farmers were able to cultivate crops or buy equipment with little, or no, initial expense. The formerly enslaved people left the plantations to form independent peasantry communities and free villages in East Dry River and Laventille.

The new peasant farmers mostly reared livestock, grew vegetables and cultivated various crops. Examples include:

• yams, cassava, corn, coconuts, bananas and peas
• sugar, cocoa and coffee
• poultry and other livestock.

As the peasant farmers produced more livestock and food, they were able to sell their extra produce at the local markets.

Opening cocoa pods, Trinidad and Tobago, c. 1900.

Exercise

1. Define peasant farming. How did peasant farmers acquire their land? Give three examples.
2. Make a list of crops grown in Trinidad and Tobago after emancipation. Find out more about one of the crops on the list. What does it look like? How is it grown?

Did you know...?

The Rada community in Belmont was formed by liberated Africans. They were freed Africans who migrated from Sierra Leone and Liberia to work as indentured servants on estates. Afterwards, they set up peasant holdings.

Women had an important role to play in peasant farming. They:

- worked alongside the men doing the farming
- looked after the animals
- carried and sold goods at market
- earned additional money for the household by taking on sewing or washing duties
- raised the children and kept the house.

Case study

Peasant farming in Toco, north Trinidad

Lord Harris was the Governor of Trinidad from 1846 to 1851 and from 1852 to 1854. In 1846, his government passed a law that authorised a new school system called the Ward School System. Under this system, in 1849, Toco in north Trinidad became a ward in the County of St David.

In his book *Trinidad: Its Geography, Natural Resources, Administration, Present Condition, and Prospects* (1858), author Louis Antoine Aimé Gaston De Verteuil recorded these observations about peasant farming in Toco:

> *The ward of Toco, in the northern division, extends along the sea-shore; this ward is entirely hilly, and parts of it of very difficult access.*
>
> *It is particularly well adapted to the cultivation of cacao, coffee, and provisions; plantains grow luxuriantly, and some of these walks on the banks of the Rio Grande, of more than sixty years' growth, are still thriving and productive, almost without culture. There was formerly, at Toco bay, a sugar estate, but it has been abandoned since emancipation.*

Research

In groups, imagine you are a peasant farmer. Research a day in the life of a 19th-century peasant farmer. Write out their daily routine, which crops they would grow and the animals they would keep.

Exercise

3. What roles did women have in peasant farming?

4. Do you think life was easier as a peasant farmer than working on a plantation or under the indenture system? Give reasons for your decision. Write 100–150 words.

Key vocabulary

migration

formerly enslaved people

peasant farming

Diversification and unification

We are learning to:

- define and apply various concepts: diversification and unification.

Changes in agricultural activities ⟩⟩

After emancipation, agriculture began to **diversify**. Further diversification also took place when the indentured labour system was ended. Diversity was an important step in the development of agriculture in Trinidad and Tobago, which for a long time had been a **monoculture** based on sugar production.

Agricultural **diversification** meant that a wider range of crops was grown across the country:

- the growing of ground provisions such as yam, cassava, dasheen
- the rearing of livestock
- the growing of vegetables such as corn and peas
- the cultivation of fruits such as cocoa, bananas and citrus.

There were several advantages to diversification:

- More and more people were able to feed and support themselves by growing their own food and raising livestock (peasant farming).
- People developed skills and experience as they started to farm new crops. This gave farmers the ability to respond to changes in the market. For example, the cacao farmers were able to produce more cacao because of the introduction of new types of cacao trees and help from experienced farmers from Venezuela.
- There was less reliance on sugar farming – so, when sugar prices collapsed or demand for sugar dropped, farmers were able to make a living from producing other crops.
- Crops were grown throughout the year, so people had food, work and income all through the year.

Cocoa Pods   *Trinidad*

Women carrying cocoa pods, Trinidad, 1897.

Exercise

1. Explain what agricultural diversification means.

2. How does diversification help with employment?

3. If you owned a small farm and you wanted to provide your family with food and a secure income throughout the year, what would you try to do? Why?

Research

Research the following benefits of agricultural diversification:

a) the links between agriculture and other industries

b) how it can create employment

c) how exporting goods can earn money for the country

d) how it can cut a country's food bill.

Write 150–200 words.

We saw in Unit 2.1 that during the 17th and 18th centuries Tobago changed hands many times between the British, French and Dutch.

In 1889, Tobago was annexed to Trinidad by the British government and the two islands were ruled as one state. The path to **unification** was a long one.

In 1833, Tobago became part of the Windward Islands along with Grenada, St Lucia, St Vincent, the Grenadines and Barbados. By the 1870s, the economic position of the Windward Islands was very serious.

- In 1876, the workers of the sugar plantations went on strike, as their working conditions had not improved much since Emancipation. On 1 May 1876, workers on the Roxborough Estate in Tobago set fire to the cane fields.
- When the police were called to arrest the workers, the crowd clashed with the police. One of the workers, Mary Jane Thomas, was accidentally killed by policeman Corporal Belmanna, who was himself beaten to death by the crowd.
- Following the Roxborough riots, the British authorities summoned a warship from Grenada to help keep the peace. The Tobago Assembly dissolved and Tobago became a Crown Colony, under British rule.
- In 1884, the sugar industry in Tobago had collapsed and British interests in the island diminished.
- In 1886, the British announced that Tobago would be annexed to Trinidad, which was completed in 1889. The islands still had some independence from each other and, in the 1890s, the British government was asked if they would consider total unification.
- Finally, in 1899, Tobago became a **ward** of the unified colony, which it remains to this day.

Exercise

4. Explain in your own words the term unification.
5. Name two of the people involved in the Roxborough riots and their role in the events.
6. Note key dates from the information you have studied and add them to your timeline.

Key vocabulary

diversify

monoculture

diversification

unification

ward

Historical data sources

We are learning to:

- Identify examples of primary and secondary sources
- Analyse primary sources of data
- Use and appreciate the variety of sources used to collect data work collaboratively.

Primary and secondary sources ⟩⟩

In Unit 1.2, we learned about **primary** and **secondary sources**. Primary sources are usually found in museums and libraries such as the National Archives of Trinidad and Tobago in Port of Spain.

Case study

National Archives of Trinidad and Tobago

The National Archives of Trinidad and Tobago is:

... the treasure-house of our country's heritage. We, at the National Archives, are the custodians of Trinidad and Tobago's memory. We acquire, preserve and make accessible thousands of records, of various formats, to the public. These include government records, immigration records, photographs, books, maps and more. Many of these records are exceptional in the way they reveal our heritage and enable us as a nation to have a better understanding of Trinidad and Tobago and our ancestors.
http://natt.gov.tt/node/2

This drawing showing Sir Walter Raleigh, a famous British explorer, in Trinidad in 1595, is an example of a primary source.

Records can be viewed if you book in advance, and there is no charge to view them. Examples of some of the things you could see include:

- A translation of a diary written in German by Friedrich Urich, a settler in Trinidad. The diary portrays what life was like in Trinidad in the period 1830–32.
- A blog on their website called *Colonial Planter* (https://nationalarchivestt.wordpress.com/) gives details of a plantation owner called Christopher Irvine and how he came to own the Strawberry Hill property on Tobago. It even shows a photograph of his tomb.

Questions

1. In your own words, explain how the National Archives help to preserve the heritage of Trinidad and Tobago.

The National Archives of Trinidad and Tobago.

2. Is the blog *Colonial Planter* a primary or secondary source? Why?

3. Working in groups, create a brochure giving information about the unification of Trinidad and Tobago. Use primary and secondary sources to collect information and draw up a timeline of events. Present your work to the rest of the class.

Types of secondary sources

In unit 1.2, we learned that a secondary source is a book or document that was created by someone who did not experience first-hand or participate in the events or conditions being researched.

This map showing the West Indies is an example of a secondary source.

Examples of secondary sources include:

- textbooks, bibliographies and biographical works
- reference books such as dictionaries, encyclopedias and atlases
- articles from journals, magazines and newspapers
- books published after the events have occurred
- history books.

Some history books that you may know about Trinidad and Tobago include:

- *A History of Modern Trinidad 1783–1962*, Professor Bridget Brereton
- *Women, Labour and Politics in Trinidad and Tobago A History*, Professor Rhoda Reddock
- *Tobago in Wartime 1798–1815*, Professor Keith O. Laurence.

These books provide an excellent source of information and analysis of the history of Trinidad and Tobago.

Did you know...?

All three history professors lectured at The University of the West Indies, St Augustine. The Alma Jordan Library at the campus has a treasure trove of primary and secondary sources on Trinidad and Tobago's history.

Exercise

Write your own definition of a primary and a secondary source.

1. Give two examples of a primary source and a secondary source in your school.

2. Working in groups of four or six, use primary and secondary sources to create a power point presentation on a historical event in Trinidad and Tobago. Make your presentation to the class.

Key vocabulary

primary source

secondary source

Historical sites

We are learning to:

- identify and describe historical sites and landmarks in the community
- investigate the origins and significance of historical sites and landmarks.

Historical sites and landmarks

Historical sites and **landmarks** are places where aspects of our political, military, cultural or social history are preserved. There are laws to protect historical sites and landmarks, because of their special heritage value.

They may be buildings, landscapes or places with interesting structures or relics. Some countries have buildings that have been standing for thousands of years, such as the Pyramids of ancient Egypt or the ruins from ancient Rome or Greece.

Examples of the different types of historical sites and landmarks in Trinidad and Tobago include:

The Red House Parliament building, Port of Spain.

- Buildings – the Red House, seat of Parliament in Trinidad and Tobago. The building was built in the late 1800s, damaged by fire in 1903 and rebuilt in 1907.
- Monuments – the Courland Monument in Tobago, built in 1976 to honour the early settlers who came from Courland (now called Latvia).
- Churches – Cathedral of the Immaculate Conception, Port of Spain, a Roman Catholic cathedral built between 1816 and 1851.
- Schools – the Queens Royal College, one of the oldest secondary schools in Trinidad and Tobago, established in 1859.
- Parks – the Matura National Park, a protected tropical forest in Trinidad.
- Landscapes – the Tobago Main Ridge Forest, the oldest forest reserve in the world. It has been protected since 1776.
- Houses – for example, Roomor and Stollmeyer's Castle.
- Cemeteries.

Stollmeyer's Castle.

Some places in Trinidad and Tobago with interesting structures or relics include:

- Fort George, built in 1804. The fort provided protection for Port of Spain.

Exercise

1. In your own words define what a historical site is.
2. Why does Trinidad and Tobago not have historical buildings from thousands of years ago?

- Fort King George, built by the British in 1777 in Tobago. It was later occupied by French troops. It was initially known as Fort King George, and later called Fort Castries. Visitors can still see the ruins of the fort, including the officers' mess, the lighthouse and the bell tower.
- Galera Point Lighthouse, next to the village of Toco, was built in 1897. It is such a popular landmark that a family park has been developed around the base.

Case study

Stollmeyer's Castle

Stollmeyer's Castle in Trinidad and Tobago was originally called Killarney, and was built by Charles Fourier Stollmeyer between 1902 and 1904. During World War II, it was occupied by American troops, and became known as The Castle. In 1979, the Government of Trinidad and Tobago bought the castle.

Research

Stollmeyer's Castle is known as one of the 'Magnificent Seven'. Do your own research using primary and secondary sources and find the other six buildings in the 'Magnificent Seven'. Find out:

- the names of the buildings
- when and where they were built
- the name of the original owners
- who owns them now
- what they are used for
- any interesting historical facts about the buildings.

Produce a brochure to highlight the origins and significance of the six other buildings. Include any interesting stories or historical details about them, along with detailed pictures or drawings.

Exercise

3. Create a timeline of the historical sites and landmarks discussed.

4. In groups, brainstorm the location of a historic site or landmark in your area, then write:

   a) what it was originally used for and what it is used for now

   b) why you think it forms an important part of our heritage.

Project

You are going to prepare a presentation about a historical site in Trinidad and Tobago to present to your class.

Each group will research and create a presentation about one of these sites: Red House, Courland Monument, Cathedral of the Immaculate Conception, Matura National Park, Fort George, Galera Point Lighthouse or Stollmeyer's Castle.

Research where it is, when it was established, what it was used for and six facts about its history. Collect photographs, draw pictures or create a poster. Then, as a group, create your presentation on your computer and present it to the class.

Key vocabulary

historical site

landmark

Comparing data sources

We are learning to:

- compare and evaluate multiple sources of information
- synthesise and draw conclusions from different sources
- value and display respect for historical sites and buildings
- work collaboratively.

Compare and evaluate multiple sources of information

It is important for researchers and students to be able to compare, contrast and evaluate information from different sources. Quite often, the full story of a particular topic does not begin to come together until you have seen or read different accounts, and you begin to draw conclusions about that topic.

We have seen that there are many different sources of primary and secondary information that we can draw from.

We can also learn from the **oral tradition** of a culture. This is where knowledge and experiences of the past are passed down the generations using spoken word, by performance poetry, storytelling or poetry recital.

Cannons at Fort King George, Scarborough, Tobago.

Respect for historical sites

It is important to be a good citizen and show respect and look after our historical sites and heritage for future generations to use. We do this by:

- protecting and preserving the historical sites
- keeping their environments clean
- having laws to protect the sites from being destroyed
- educating the public about the heritage of the sites
- having field trips to historical sites.

Research

Choose a historical site that you want to know more about. Interview some elders in your community, and find out from them what the area looked like when they were young and how people used it. Write a report about the way the area has changed.

Activity

Write a reflective piece in your journal in which you imagine living in one of the places you have visited or read about. Imagine what life was like there and what your daily routine would be like. How different would it be to your routine today?

Case study

The Roxborough Riots, 1876

The internet is often the first place you would go to if you wanted to research a topic. However, when you search on the web for a topic, you often come up with many different results. For example, if you were to search 'Roxborough Riots, 1876', an internet search can show over 600 results. Often, you have to be selective with the results at the top of the list. For example:

- Encyclopedia.com gives a summary of the events.
- The National Archives of Trinidad and Tobago has a blog titled '1876 Labour Riot in Tobago', which gives a bit more detail. It also quotes from 'Post-Emancipation Protest in the Caribbean: The "Roxborough Riots" in Tobago, 1876', an article that gives a first-hand account of the standoff in the Roxborough courthouse.

Other suggestions for sources you could use to research the Roxborough Riots include:

- Visiting the National Archives of Trinidad and Tobago in Port of Spain, which has most of the newspapers published in Trinidad and Tobago from 1825 to 2007. Some of the titles they hold include the *Port of Spain Gazette* (1825–1956) and the *Trinidad Chronicle* (1864–1959). You could research how the newspapers reported the events.
- Going to the Parliament Library in Port of Spain. Here they hold copies of the *Trinidad Royal Gazette* from 1874, along with official documents.
- Visiting the site of the riots in Roxborough and see what information there is at the actual location.
- History books in your local library and in school.
- Interviewing people in the community who may know about the Roxborough Riots.

Project

In groups, you are going to research the Roxborough Riots of 1876. Use primary and secondary sources to put together a brochure about the events of the riots. Use some of the ideas above for your research. When you have gathered all the information together, write a fictional newspaper report of the events of 3 May 1876, using any photos and drawings that you have found. Write 150–200 words. Then present your project to the class.

Key vocabulary

oral tradition

Historical events

We are learning to:

- examine the historical factors that have contributed to the social development of the community
- examine the impact of historical events such as slavery, indentureship and inter-island migration.

Impact of slavery

What was the impact on the communities in Trinidad and Tobago of some of these historical events that we have been looking at? Trinidad and Tobago today is famous for its **racial** and **cultural diversity**, which means that people from many different backgrounds make up our population.

The origins of this can be traced back to the colonial era, with the arrival of enslaved people from Africa, and then later indentureship and inter-island migration. As a result, we have a large number of different languages and cultural traditions that come from countries all over the world. For example:

- Religion – practices that can be recognised in Obeah, voodoo and Shango.
- Language – the Caribbean invented a common language. This led to the emergence of patois (a mixture of African, French, English and Spanish dialects).
- Food – for example, yam, cocoa, asham, fufu.
- Music – for example, Congo talking drum, abeng, xylophone, bamboo fife.

The graph shows the different ethnic groups that make up our population today.

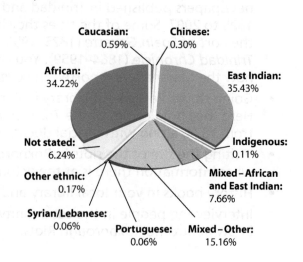

Caucasian: 0.59%
Chinese: 0.30%
African: 34.22%
East Indian: 35.43%
Not stated: 6.24%
Indigenous: 0.11%
Other ethnic: 0.17%
Mixed – African and East Indian: 7.66%
Syrian/Lebanese: 0.06%
Portuguese: 0.06%
Mixed – Other: 15.16%

Exercise

1. What does each number on the pie chart represent?
2. What are the two largest ethnic groups in Trinidad and Tobago?
3. Look back through this unit. How many of the ethnic groups came to Trinidad and Tobago through slavery or indentureship, and are they shown in the pie chart above?

Activity

Write a poem or short story describing some of the changes discussed in communities on this page.

Impact of indentureship >>>

Indentureship impacted on Trinidad and Tobago society demographically, economically and culturally.

- Demographically – by 1861, the total population of Trinidad was 50% immigrants. Over time, this would have a significant impact on the cultural diversity of the island. As the immigrants began work on the estates, other immigrant groups moved into other work, such as shopkeepers and market gardening, and professional jobs such as teachers, clergy or public servants.

- Economically – the sugar industry needed the additional labour. The immigrants helped to increase the number of workers on the estates, which eventually led to an increase in productivity and exports. After indentureship, the Indian people also grew crops such as rice bodi and watermelons for domestic use. They also reared animals. Any surplus was sold in the local markets.

- Culturally – Trinidad and Tobago became more culturally diverse because of the movement of people; for example, there were different religions, languages and food.

Impact of inter-island migration >>>

Inter-island migration is the process of moving from one country to another country; for example, from Jamaica to Trinidad. After emancipation, people began moving within the Caribbean region, often to Trinidad, in search of work and better working and living conditions. Some of these migrants came from Grenada, St Vincent and Barbados.

The impact of inter-island migration on Trinidad and Tobago is similar to that of the impact of slavery and indentureship – the economic and cultural impacts were similar.

One lasting effect of inter-island migration was the eventual formation of CARICOM in 1973, which allowed movement of people between CARICOM countries.

Cane cutting in Trinidad, circa 1930.

Exercise

4. In your own words, explain how indentureship impacted on Trinidad and Tobago.

5. Explain the term inter-island migration.

6. Why do you think Trinidad and Tobago started to become culturally diverse from 1861? (clue: immigration)

Key vocabulary

racial diversity

cultural diversity

Women and the community

We are learning to:

- compare and contrast the social development of various communities: emergent issues of gender.

Issues of gender ›››

Life for enslaved African women in the 19th century was a very difficult and dangerous one. Initially, they were captured in their homeland in Africa and brought over to Trinidad to work on a plantation.

Once there, they would work in the fields, preparing the land, planting, doing the harvest, and transporting and milling the same cane. Some worked as domestic staff in the plantation owner's house, but this was hard work too, and frequently the women were subjected to sexual abuse.

Workers sit on the ground with baskets in a cocoa plantation, 1897.

After emancipation ›››

After emancipation in 1838, the formerly enslaved people would take up peasant farming. This was not easy work either, and sometimes women would have to work on other plantations doing manual work to supplement the family's income. The educational system gradually began to improve for women, and sometimes they could study subjects such as sewing and housekeeping.

After indentureship ››››

After indentureship, women continued to grow crops and rear animals, while others worked as cane cutters or labourers, and they would earn less than the men for doing the same work. Educational opportunities were few, though some women did take courses in dressmaking and flower arranging.

Exercise

1. In your own words, explain why life was difficult for women in the 19th century.

2. How did women who worked as peasant farmers supplement their income?

3. What subjects were open for women to study?

Did you know...?

In 1995, the United Nations (UN) Security Council stated that: "The equal access and full participation of women in power structures and their full involvement in all efforts for the prevention and resolution of conflicts are essential for the maintenance and promotion of peace and security."

Today, in most countries, women and men are equal under the law. They have the same rights, meaning there is what we call **gender equality**.

In the late 19th to mid-20th century, women faced discrimination with regard to education, employment and political rights throughout the Caribbean.

For many working-class families, with less money available, access to education was restricted – some children needed to work on family agricultural plots. Many only attended primary or elementary schools as most secondary schools were fee-paying schools. The curricula at secondary school was different for girls than for boys – boys were given the opportunity to apply for the island scholarship to attend university.

In some jobs, women were paid less than men. To be able to vote, both men and women had to have certain income and property qualifications. Women also had to be 30 years old to vote. In 1925, women in Trinidad were not permitted to stand for election to the Legislative Council.

Today, there have been some changes in Trinidad's society that offer help and protection for women. These include:

- Women's rights – women now have much greater opportunities in education and employment, have laws to protect them against discrimination (for instance, the Maternity Protection Bill, 1997) and laws to protect them in social and family situations (the Domestic Violence Act, 1999, for example).

- Greater educational opportunities – in the past, more money was invested in male education, but this has changed, with more women moving into higher education.

- More women working – as opportunities have increased in education, so have the opportunities for educated women to work in roles that previously were reserved for men.

Research

The organisation Women Working for Social Progress is based in Port of Spain and works to raise issues affecting women in society. Research its role and activities, and write 150–200 words on its contribution to gender equality.

Exercise

4. Name three organisations in society today that offer help and protection for women.

5. Give three ways in which women were discriminated against in the 19th to mid 20th century.

6. Do you think that gender issues only affect women, or do they affect everyone?

7. Do you agree or disagree with the United Nations' statement about gender equality? Explain your point of view.

Key vocabulary

gender equality

The need for reform

We are learning to:

- compare and contrast the social development of various communities: emergent issues of race.

The need for reform

The **constitution** of Trinidad and Tobago guarantees certain rights to citizens. The constitution states that these rights are given "without **discrimination** by reason of **race**, origin, colour, religion or sex".

Lord Harris, the Governor of Trinidad 1846–51 and 1852–4, helped to bring new immigrants to Trinidad, but he realised that certain reforms were going to be needed if the immigrants and formerly enslaved people were to have a part in society in Trinidad. In 1848, he declared that "a race has been freed, but a society has not been formed (in Trinidad)". Trinidad and Tobago has a long history of its citizens' fight for their rights.

Steel drum players at Carnival, Trinidad.

Canboulay Riots, 1881

Following emancipation, the formerly enslaved people would celebrate their freedom by having a festival on 1 August each year. Later, the celebration joined the Carnival. Canboulays were processions during Carnival that celebrated the harvesting of burned cane fields during slavery.

The British authorities disapproved of the Carnival and abolished the parade in 1881. This was seen as an attempt to deny black citizens their rights in a free society. Riots took place in Port of Spain and there were serious disturbances between the police and rioters.

The incident caused deep resentment within Trinidadian society towards the British government. This worsened when the government banned drumming in 1883 and then stick fighting in 1884. Today, the Canboulay celebrations are still part of Carnival.

> **Did you know...?**
>
> In the Hosein Massacre in 1884, hundreds of people defied government ordinance to protest through the streets of San Fernando. Police fired on the crowd leaving 11 dead and hundreds injured.

Exercise

1. Why did Lord Harris say that social reforms were needed in the 19th century?

2. Explain in your own words why the government tried to ban the Canboulay celebrations.

3. Explain in your own words the terms discrimination and race.

The 1970 army mutiny and Bloody Tuesday

At the start of the 1970s, **Black Power** ideology swept across America and the Caribbean. The movement was made up mostly of young people of African descent. The Black Power movement started in Trinidad and Tobago with the aim of:

- ending all injustice and oppression faced by people of colour in society
- ensuring equal employment rights
- ending foreign influence in the country
- improving the status of African culture in society.

In 1970, there were demonstrations against the government in several towns. Police and soldiers were called in to stop the demonstrations. There was violence, which led to bigger and bigger demonstrations.

There were nightly meetings in Woodford Square, which became known as the People's Parliament. Many members of the police and army also supported the demonstrators.

The government then declared a **state of emergency**.

People were not allowed to move around at night and leaders of the rebellion were arrested. Then two lieutenants in the army, Raffique Shah and Rex Lassalle, led an army **mutiny.** Police and soldiers who were loyal to the government brought the situation under control and the mutineers were arrested, tried in court martials (military courts) and put in jail.

This proved ineffective, as the unrest and the state of emergency continued for several months. In 1975, there were strikes in the oil, sugar, transport and electricity sectors, which paralysed the country.

A march involving tens of thousands of people took place on Tuesday 18 March 1975. This march for 'Peace, Bread and Justice' was to go from San Fernando to Port of Spain. The police were sent in to stop the marchers. They used tear gas and batons and many people were injured and beaten. This became known as 'Bloody Tuesday'.

Questions

1. Explain briefly what the Black Power movement was and list its aims.

2. Why do you think people were attracted to the Black Power movement?

3. Create a timeline of the events in Trinidad we have just discussed. Add notes to your dates.

Black Power leader Geddes Granger addresses a huge crowd during a demonstration in March 1970.

> **Did you know...?**
>
> The term Black Power is usually associated with the American civil rights leader Stokely Carmichael.

Research

Using primary and secondary sources, research either the Black Power movement in Trinidad or the events leading up to Bloody Tuesday. Use pictures and write 100–150 words.

Key vocabulary

constitution

discrimination

race

Black Power

state of emergency

mutiny

Society in the 20th century

We are learning to:

- compare and contrast the social development of various communities: emergent issues of class.

Unrest and strikes in the 1930s

Class is the division of people in a society into groups according to their social status; for example, upper class, middle class and working class. The 1930s saw a big change for the **working classes** in Trinidad and Tobago. From the early 20th century, the sugar industry had been in decline and, although the new oil industry in Trinidad was profitable, the wages for the working class were low and the oil companies exploited the workers.

Workers were not allowed to strike, and very few workers had **political franchise** in the 1930s. In order to be eligible to vote for members of the Legislative Council, a person had to own property or have a high income. The interests of workers were therefore not represented in government.

Other factors also began to contribute to unrest among workers:

- a lot of unemployment and underemployment
- trade unions were not recognised
- lower wages, but costs of living increased
- employers and colonial government officials still displayed racist and arrogant attitudes towards workers.

Workers wanted better working conditions, respect and the freedom to protest if necessary. This led to the development of trade unions and political parties. All these factors led to unrest in many other Caribbean countries. Eventually, the laws were changed so that the rights of workers were respected and they had more freedom and protection. The timeline opposite shows the events.

Exercise

1. What factors contributed to the unrest amongst the working classes?

2. What did workers do in Trinidad in 1934?

3. Why do you think there was labour unrest on Trinidad?

1934: Hunger March to Port of Spain; demonstrations and violence on several sugar estates

1935: Strike on oilfields and bigger hunger march to Port of Spain

1935: Government sets up a Wages Advisory Board

1936: T.U.B. Butler launches own party

1937: T.U.B. Butler organises strike at Trinidad Leaseholds Limited oilfields; strike spreads to other oilfields and becomes general strike; state of emergency declared; calm restored; some support for workers from Governor and Colonial Secretary

Trade unions

As a result of the unrest in the 1930s, and in particular the unrest in 1937, the British government conceded that the workers were being exploited by their employers. The British government then agreed that **trade unions** would be recognised.

The role of the trade unions was to be a strong 'voice' for the working class in Trinidad and Tobago, and would ensure that workers were paid and treated fairly.

Important early trade unions included:

- the Oilfields Workers' Trade Union (OWTU)
- the All Trinidad Sugar Estates and Factory Workers Trade Union (ATEFWTU)
- the Federated Workers Trade Union (FWTU).

Both the OWTU and the ATEFWTU were founded by Adrian Cola Rienzi in 1937. In 1938, the Trinidad Labour Department was set up to mediate in disputes between the employers and the trade unions.

T.U.B. Butler (1897–1977)

Tubal Uriah 'Buzz' Butler, or 'Comrade Chief Servant' as he was also known, was a key figure in mobilising the workers to protest about their poor working conditions.

He organised hunger marches in 1934 and 1935 and the first proper strike on the oilfields in 1935. Demonstrations were peaceful until the police tried to stop them. People were killed and injured, and Butler was arrested and imprisoned for two years in 1937. A few years later, he was arrested again after organising another strike.

Butler served as a member of the Legislative Council from 1950 to 1961. In 1970, he was awarded the Trinity Cross.

Exercise

4. What role did T.U.B. Butler play in bringing about changes in Trinidad and Tobago in the 1930s? How important were these changes?

5. Do you think strikes and rebellions are the best way to bring about change in your country?

6. Add the most important dates from this period to your timeline.

1938: Trinidad Labour Department established after investigations by British government into causes of unrest

1939: World War II breaks out

Project

The Trinidadian writer Samuel Selvon published a collection of short stories called *Ways of Sunlight* in 1957. The stories detail what it was like to live in 1930s multicultural Trinidadian society. Your teacher will help you either research about the book or find a copy for you. Read three or four of the stories and summarise what life was like in Trinidad.

Key vocabulary

class

working class

political franchise

trade union

The diversity of our community

We are learning to:

- value the diversity of various communities.

The diversity of communities ⟩⟩

We have seen in this unit the impact slavery, indentureship and inter-island migration had on the economic, religious and cultural life of Trinidad and Tobago.

The immigrants who came to live in Trinidad and Tobago brought their own religions and cultural practices with them, which resulted in a **multicultural society**.

Today Trinidad and Tobago has become a place of great cultural diversity that we can value. Our people come from Africa, Europe and India, with many different ethnicities, languages, religions and cultural traditions.

A local market in Scarborough, Tobago.

These different influences have met and mixed in Trinidad and Tobago, with the result that we have many communities. Each community, though, is different and depends on a number of factors, such as:

- its origin, history and location – for example, whether the community was set up after emancipation, after people had bought themselves out of indentureship or as a result of inter-island immigration or migrants from other parts of Trinidad and Tobago
- characteristics of the community, such as its population and composition of ethnicity, religion, gender, age and language – for example, English, French, Creole, Arabic and Bhojpuri
- its settlement patterns and use of land – for example, how much of the land is used for housing, sugar cane, crops, pasture or not used at all
- economic and employment activities
- institutions and public services
- educational services – for example, some schools in some communities may be religious schools, such as Presbyterian
- cultural activities and traditions, including arts and music, cuisine and dress.

Activity

Create a mind map showing the different factors that make up a community. Add examples to each one.

Religious practices

Trinidad and Tobago is a multi-religious country, which means that there are many different religious practices in the country. The religious practices of a community are dependent on which religion the community follows. For example:

- Christianity celebrates Easter.
- Hindus celebrate Diwali, Phagwa.
- Islam celebrates Eid-al-Fitr, the Hosay Festival.

Cultural activities and traditions

Each community has different traditions and festivals – for example, the religious festivals outlined above – but they can share non-religious festivals such as Indian Arrival Day, which commemorates the arrival of East Indian indentured labourers to work on the plantations (30 May each year), and Emancipation Day, which commemorates the abolition of slavery and the freeing of all enslaved people in Trinidad and Tobago (1 August each year).

The Parade of Bands, Port of Spain, 2017.

Other diverse cultural aspects include:

- different types of cuisine (food), such as roti and curried mango (Indian), pelau (Spanish) and bamboo shoots and tea (Chinese)
- different types of traditional dress, such as the Indian sari
- music and dance – calypso, soca and rumba (all originating from Africa); dances like the Kuchipudi (Indian), lion and ribbon dances (Chinese), and African orisha dance movements
- folklore – stories about Anansi (originally from Africa) and Papa Bois (from French Caribbean culture).

Discussion

In pairs or groups, discuss the various activities and traditions that exist in Trinidadian culture. Use the information on these pages and make a list of how many you have in your own community.

Exercise

1. Name a religious festival celebrated by:

   a) Christians

   b) Hindus

   c) Muslims.

2. Name five factors that help to explain why each community is different in Trinidad and Tobago.

3. You are going to do a project about your community. Take the five factors you identified in question 4, and write notes about what happens in your community in relation to these. You can add photos from the internet or your own drawings. Write about 300 words.

Key vocabulary

multicultural society

Life in the village and the city

We are learning to:

- compare and contrast the economic development of various communities, life in the village vs life in the city
- appreciate the history of their community
- use primary and secondary sources to create a digital story (narrative) about the community.

Economic development ≫

Trinidad and Tobago moved from a sugar-based economy in the 19th century to an oil-based economy in the 20th century. This shift resulted in much of the population moving from a **rural** to an **urban** environment. This is known as **internal migration**.

In Trinidad the developing oil industry pulled many people to urban areas in search of work. Low wages in agricultural jobs, combined with the new oil industry and emerging jobs in construction and manufacturing, made the rural life less appealing.

A **village** is a human-made environment mostly made up of family homes, although it may have a small central area with some shops and community buildings such as a police station, clinic and church. In farming areas, a village may have only a few tarred roads. Jobs are more agriculturally based.

A **city** is a large settlement where people live and work and is made up of businesses such as shops, malls, industrial buildings such as warehouses and factories, and a transport infrastructure such as roads, train tracks, bus and train stations, airports, roads, harbour and port facilities. People often work in the city centre and live in the suburbs, so they have to commute to work by bus, car or train. Schools, health care and even entertainment are better in urban areas.

A view of the waterfront at Port of Spain, Trinidad.

Exercise

1. What are the two products that Trinidad and Tobago economy has been (and is) based on?

2. In your own words, define the terms village, city and internal migration.

3. In your own words, explain the differences between a village and a city. Write about 100 words.

Life in the village and the city ▶▶▶

There are a number of differences between living in a rural community, such as a village, and in an urban area, such as a city. For example, in urban areas:

- there is better housing
- utilities, such as water and electricity, are better
- there are more job opportunities
- the transport infrastructure is better developed
- there are better schools and colleges in urban areas
- there are more health care facilities in urban areas.

There are some disadvantages to living in urban areas:

Village life in Lopinot Village, Trinidad.

- Housing and everyday living costs are more expensive.
- Social problems such as teenage pregnancy, street children, substance abuse, child abuse is in greater numbers in urban areas.
- There is more pollution than in rural areas.
- People don't know each other as well, there is less of a community feel, and people are less appreciative of community history and cultural heritage.

Project

You are going to do a project comparing life in a village and life in a city. Choose a village and city close to where you live. Think about some of the things listed above and do some research to compare what life is like. You should also consider economic and employment activities, how land is used and whether people are better off financially in a village or a city (think about how much people earn and how much they have to spend).

Use primary and secondary sources to help your investigation and, if possible, interview community members for their views on whether they would prefer to live in a village or a city. Use the internet, newspapers and magazines to illustrate your project. Use a T-chart, like the one below, to compare your village and city.

When you have finished your research, write a reflective piece to answer the question 'I would prefer to live in a village/city because…' Write about 250 words.

Village	City

Key vocabulary

rural

urban

internal migration

village

city

Development of industries

We are learning to:

- examine the historical factors that have contributed to the economic development of the community, introduction and development of industries, e.g. sugar, rice, cocoa, oil.

The sugar industry

The sugar industry has a long history in Trinidad and Tobago. The timeline below summarises the key points:

- Dutch settlers planted sugar cane in 1630 in Trinidad.
- From 1783, French settlers planted more cane.
- The arrival of the British in 1797 turned the island into a large-scale sugar colony. The sugar industry was able to develop because of the work of the enslaved African people that the British brought to the island.
- After emancipation in 1838, sugar production dropped because of a shortage of labour and because the owners now had to pay wages to the labourers. This led to indentureship.
- When indentureship ended, the Indian immigrants left the big plantations to become small independent sugar farmers. By 1902, more than half the sugar produced on Trinidad was produced by these independent farmers.
- After World War I, sugar prices fell because of competition from sugar beet and cheap imports from Cuba and the East Indies. Farms began to close.
- To help create jobs, in 1975 the government bought up all the sugar farms that still existed and formed a company called Caroni (1975) Limited. Caroni then started on a programme of diversification to make use of all the land, including dairy farming, buffalypso farming, and the growing of rice, coffee, citrus and other fruit like pineapples and pawpaws.
- In 2003, Caroni was closed, as it had been heavily subsidised by the government for many years.

Migrant workers cutting sugar cane on a plantation in Trinidad, c. 1897.

Exercise

1. How did sugar farming change after emancipation?

2. How did the government help the people of Trinidad and Tobago when it created Caroni (1975) Limited?

3. Find three important dates in the information you have studied and add them to your timeline.

Activity

Your teacher will organise a field trip to the museum of the Sugar Heritage Village. Before you go on the trip, work in groups and make a list of the questions you think you will be able to find answers to at the museum. Record your answers and use them to give feedback to the class after the trip.

The cocoa industry ▶▶▶

The first cacao trees were planted in Trinidad by the Spanish in 1525. By 1830, Trinidad and Tobago had become the world's third-largest producer of cacao after Venezuela and Ecuador, producing 20% of the world's cacao. After emancipation, some formerly enslaved people began to grow cacao and farmers from Venezuela also came to the country to farm it. Cacao farming continued to be the most important part of the economy until the 1920s, when a series of factors caused the decline of the industry:

- West African countries, such as Ghana, started to produce large quantities of cacao.
- World War I disrupted trade.
- Diseases like Witches' Broom Disease destroyed crops.
- There was a worldwide depression.

Today, there are estimated to be more than 3000 farms in Trinidad and Tobago that produce cacao. These farms are mainly in the north, where the soil and climate are ideal for cacao farming.

The oil industry ▶▶▶▶

Some of the first oil wells in the world were drilled in Trinidad. When commercial production was established, petroleum replaced agriculture as the mainstay of the economy. In the 1970s, sales of petroleum accounted for as much as 90% of export earnings. Later, natural gas became more important than petroleum. Diversification into the production of steel, petrochemicals and iron was made possible by the country's vast mineral resources. The timeline shows the main events.

Exercise

4. Who introduced cacao to Trinidad and Tobago?
5. Why did the cacao industry decline in the 1920s? Give two reasons.
6. Where was oil first discovered and produced commercially?
7. What disrupted oil production in the 1930s?
8. When did the government start to buy oil companies?
9. Work in groups and research the crops grown after emancipation. Find out more about the production of cacao. Where were the first farms? Where are the farms today? Where was cacao exported? How much was exported? What was the contract system? Find out about other crops, like coconuts, vegetables and coffee. Where were these grown? Were they exported or sold at local markets?

2.15

Timeline of key events in history of oil and petroleum:

| 1857: First oil well drilled by Merrimac Company near Pitch Lake |

| 1908: Commercial production begins near Pitch Lake, La Brea |

| 1910: First cargo of oil exported |

| 1920s: Oil exports become significant |

| 1937: Labour unrest disrupts production |

| 1939–45: World War II disruptions, but oil industry booms |

| 1958: Offshore oil drilling begins |

| 1969: Government of Trinidad and Tobago acquires first oil company (part of British Petroleum) |

| 1973: World oil prices rise; Trinidad experiences an oil boom |

| 1980–present: Government of Trinidad and Tobago signs a number of production-sharing contracts with private companies |

The economic development of a community is linked to individuals, their skills sets and their history. For example, the community of Lopinot is known for its contribution to the cocoa industry; Caroni and St. Madeline are known for the sugar industry; and the communities of LaBrea, Point Fortin and Barrackpore are known for their links to the oil industry.

Rice cultivation

Rice cultivation in Trinidad is linked to the settlement of two groups of people – the Merikins, who cultivated dry rice (*Oryza glaberrima*) and the ex-indentured Indian labourers, who cultivated lagoon or paddy rice. The Merikins were freed Africans who had fought for the British in 1812 and were consequently awarded land in Princes Town, New Grant and Moruga by the British government. The ex-indentured Indians cultivated rice mainly in the areas of Caroni swamp and Oropouche lagoon.

Rice in the hands of a worker

Rice cultivation is important to both groups: for the Merikins, it is part of their oral history tradition; for the Indians, it is part of their religion and culture. It is symbolic of prosperity and is used in various Hindu ceremonies and rituals.

Rice was originally cultivated in Trinidad as a food source for the Indian and Merikin communities; it helped to make both more self-sufficient. It was not until the 1980s, with the diversification of the Caroni (1975) Ltd company, that paddy rice was cultivated for both export and domestic use. Today, the rice industry in Trinidad is represented by both dry rice and paddy rice. Dry rice cultivation has mechanised and a formal company, Vista Dorado Estates, has been established, but only serves the domestic market. Paddy rice is produced for both domestic and foreign markets. A recent development here is the opening of a rice parboiling plant in Couva.

Activity

1. Group work: In groups or 4 or 6 conduct interviews with rice growers on the process of rice cultivation. Using the information collected, along with photos, make a power point presentation. Each group share their findings with the class.

2. Find out more about the production of dry and paddy rice. Write a short report (130–150 words) on the advantages and disadvantages of each method of production. State which one you prefer, giving reasons for your answers.

Discussion

Class Debate: Divide the class into two teams. Debate the following motion:

Be it resolved that in light of the growing concern for nutrition, food security, climate change and being self sufficient, paddy rice cultivation is the best option.

Each team should have three speakers. One team should propose the motion and the other should oppose it.

Questions

See how well you have understood the topics in this unit.

1. Match the key vocabulary word (i–v) with its definition (a–e).

   i) colonialism

   ii) colony

   iii) Crown Colony

   iv) indentureship

   v) emancipation

   a) gaining control over land in another country and exploiting its wealth

   b) the removal of restraint or restrictions on an individual or a group of people

   c) a country under the control of another country

   d) contract labour with harsh conditions

   e) a country ruled by the monarch of another country

2. What bill came into effect on 1 August 1834?

3. What took place on the Roxborough Estate in Tobago in 1876? Explain the events in 50 words.

4. Give two examples of a primary source and two examples of a secondary source.

5. Using primary and secondary sources, complete a short descriptive piece (150–175 words) on the Hosein Massacre 1884. Clearly define the following: reasons for the Hosein celebrations, events of the day, the outcome and your thoughts on how the event was handled by the colonial authorities.

6. What would you find in the National Archives of Trinidad and Tobago?

7. What type of historical landmark is the Red House?

8. Which historical site is being described?

   _____ in Trinidad and Tobago was originally called Killarney, and was built...between 1902 and 1904. During World War II, it was occupied by American troops, and became known as The Castle.

9. How can we show respect for our historical sites?

10. Explain why it is important to preserve historical landmarks and buildings in our community.

11. Imagine you were a student in early 20th century Trinidad and Tobago. Write a reflective piece on:

    i) your access to education

    ii) your prospects of finding a job or attending university after leaving school

    iii) your right to political representation as an adult.

12. Explain briefly what happened at the Canboulay Riots in 1881.

13. Name three important trade unions that were formed in Trinidad and Tobago in the 1930s.

14. Match these events with the dates.

   i) State of emergency declared

   ii) Strike on oilfields and second hunger march to Port of Spain

   iii) T.U.B. Butler launches own party

   iv) Trinidad Labour Department established after investigations by British government into causes of unrest

   v) Hunger March to Port of Spain

   a) 1934

   b) 1935

   c) 1936

   d) 1937

   e) 1938

15. Name three factors that help make each community in Trinidad and Tobago different.

16. Trinidad and Tobago is made up of many ethnic groups. Make a brochure defining your ethnic group. Include your religion, language, music, cuisine and dress.

17. A mind map is a diagram used to visually organise information. It shows the relationship between pieces of information, and can include images. Create a mind map on how the sugar industry in Trinidad has evolved between 1630 and 2003.

18. Match these events to their dates in the history of petroleum in Trinidad and Tobago.

   i) first oil well drilled near Pitch Lake

   ii) commercial production begins

   iii) first cargo of oil exported

   iv) labour unrest disrupts production

   v) offshore oil drilling begins

   vi) world oil prices rise; Trinidad experiences an oil boom

   a) 1908

   b) 1857

   c) 1973

   d) 1910

   e) 1937

   f) 1958

19. In your own words, explain what happened with the army mutiny in 1970 and on Bloody Tuesday. Write your account in the style of a newspaper report.

20. Define the terms colonialism and Crown Colony, and explain how they relate to Trinidad and Tobago.

21. Write a short essay explaining how indentureship started in Trinidad and Tobago. Outline the problems with indentureship that led to the end of the system in the early 20th century. Write about 250 words.

22. Why was there migration of ex-slaves and ex-indentured servants within Trinidad and Tobago in the aftermath of emancipation and immigration?

23. Explain the advantages of agricultural diversification in the 19th century in Trinidad and Tobago.

24. You are going to research the Roxborough riots of 1876 and the role of Mary Jane Thomas and Corporal Belmanna. What primary sources do you think you will need. List them and then do the research. Write 100–150 words.

25. Write a newspaper report that outlines the unrest and strikes that took place in Trinidad and Tobago in the 1930s. Describe the events and people involved.

26. Create a mind map or graphic organiser which shows the differences between living in a rural community and living in an urban area.

27. Explain the role of the sugar industry in the economic development of Trinidad and Tobago.

28. In 75 to 100 words define some of the challenges faced by the sugar industry in Trinidad and Tobago.

29. Why is rice cultivation important to the Merikins and the East Indian people of Trinidad and Tobago?

30. How has rice cultivation developed in Trinidad from the 19th century to the present day?

31. What is oral tradition?

32. What knowledge do you think can be passed on from one generation to the next by oral sources?

Checking your progress

To make good progress in understanding your community, check to make sure you understand these ideas.

Explain that colonialism and being a Crown Colony played a significant part in Trinidad and Tobago's history.

Explain the impact the transatlantic slave trade and emancipation had on Trinidad and Tobago.

Explain the path to the unification of Trinidad and Tobago.

Name examples of primary sources.

Explain how the National Archives help to preserve the heritage of Trinidad and Tobago.

Create a brochure using primary and secondary sources on a topic.

Identify different types of historical sites in Trinidad and Tobago.

Examine the impact of slavery, indentureship and inter-island migration on our community.

Examine how we value the diversity of various communities in Trinidad and Tobago.

Examine the historical factors that have contributed to the economic development of the community.

Name the industries which have contributed to the nation's economic development.

Complete a project comparing life in a village and life in a city.

HISTORY

Unit 3: History of my country Trinidad and Tobago

In this unit you will find out ⟩⟩⟩

Indigenous people and the Europeans

- The indigenous people of Trinidad and Tobago
  - migratory patterns, pre-European contact before 1492, location
- Experiences and contribution of the indigenous people
- The early European presence on Tobago's development
- Economic and political experiences of Tobago and Trinidad in the 1800s
- Economic and political experiences of Trinidad and Tobago in the 19th and 20th centuries
  - economic development, slavery, emancipation, apprenticeship, metayage, peasantry
  - the role of key figures during the period
- The functioning of the THA
  - structure and function, quest for self-government

Challenges to the social order: trade unionism and social activism

- Key figures and groups in trade unionism and social activism 1900–1970
  - Tubal Uriah 'Buzz' Butler, Adrian 'Cola' Rienzi, George Weekes
  - Negro Welfare Cultural and Social Association (NWCSA), Trinidad Working Men's Association (TWA), Oilfield Workers' Trade Union (OWTU)
  - Audrey Jeffers, Clothil Walcott
  - Water Riots 1903; Labour Riots 1930

Challenges to the social order: the Black Power Movement, 1970

- The causes and consequences, motivation and struggles, individuals and groups of the Black Power Movement

The West Indian Federation

- The factors which led to the establishment of the Federation, its achievements and what contributed to its failure

Independence

- Key figures in the independence movement
  - Dr Eric Eustace Williams, Rudranath Capildeo, Albert Gomes

Indigenous people of Trinidad and Tobago

We are learning to:

- outline the presence of the indigenous people of Trinidad and Tobago: migratory patterns.

The first indigenous people of Trinidad and Tobago

The **first people** of Trinidad and Tobago were the **Amerindians,** who settled on the islands roughly 18 000 years ago. First people are the first known population of a place, usually indigenous people.

About 18 000 years ago, the Amerindians began to migrate from their original settlements in Siberia, crossed over the Bering Straits and moved into Alaska and then moved south through North, Central, and South America. During their movement southwards, some of the Amerindians established settlements and formed indigenous tribes, while the others moved further south.

The Caribs and Arawaks

Between 2 000 and 2 500 years ago a new group of Amerindians travelled to Trinidad and Tobago from Venezuela. These were the **Caribs** (or Kalinago tribe) and **Arawaks** (or the Taino tribe).

The Caribs lived in the north and west of Trinidad in settlements like Arima and Mucurapo. The Arawaks lived in the southeast and in Tobago. The Arawaks were a peaceful tribe, who were often attacked by the more warlike Caribs. Both established their settlements along the coast, near rivers and at the top of hills.

Trinidad and Tobago at the time of Columbus' arrival

By the time Columbus arrived in Trinidad in 1498, the islands had a population of around 40 000 **indigenous** Amerindians. Some of the population spoke the Arawak language, while others spoke Cariban.

Exercise

1. What do you understand by the word indigenous?
2. Name the two tribes that came to Trinidad and Tobago from Venezuela.
3. Where did the new tribes settle?

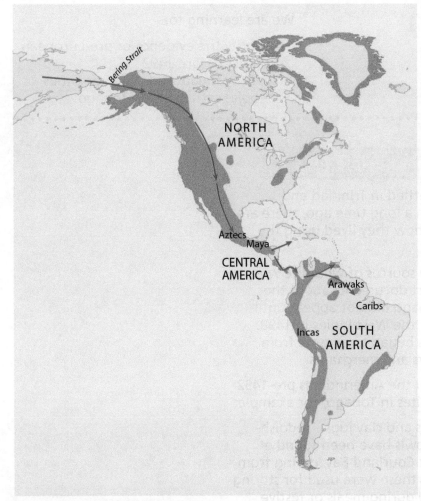

The migratory route of the Amerindians.

The indigenous Amerindians' food came from crops such as cassava, maize, potatoes, tomatoes, beans and fruits. They also fished and hunted animals.

Cotton was grown to make clothes and bedding, as well as tobacco, which they smoked or chewed. The name Tobago comes from the word tobacco, which shows how important this crop was to them.

Project

Trace the map shown on this page and add the route our Amerindian ancestors took to get to Trinidad and Tobago and the dates they did it. Then, trace a map of Trinidad and Tobago and add the new settlements of the Kalingos and the Tainos, together with the food they grew there.

Exercise

4. Explain in your own words, the route our Amerindian ancestors took to get to Trinidad and Tobago.

5. What crops did the new settlers grow?

6. Where does the name Tobago come from?

7. How do we get the term Amerindian?

Key vocabulary

first people

Amerindians

Caribs

Arawaks

indigenous

Pre-European contact

We are learning to:

- identify the evidence of pre-European contact before 1492
- identify the location of indigenous peoples settlement in Tobago.

Evidence of pre-European contact before 1492

Even though the Amerindians settled in Trinidad and Tobago and the wider Caribbean a long time ago, there are still many ways we can discover how they lived using the evidence they left behind.

There are very few documentary sources of what life was like for the Amerindians. The first documents about the Amerindians in Trinidad and Tobago did not appear until the third voyage of Columbus to the West Indies in 1498. After this other written accounts began to emerge from explorers, fortune hunters, sailors and merchants.

Evidence of what life was like for the Amerindians pre-1492 can be found at archaeological sites in Tobago, for example:

- **Artefacts** such as bowls, pots and clay jugs – reddish-brown, fine-ware pottery bowls have been found at archaeological sites at Great Courland Bay, dating from AD 1150–1400. Bowls such as these were used for storing and presenting beer or food during meals or festive communal and inter-village gatherings. Examples of this type of pottery are exhibited in the Tobago Historical Museum, Scarborough.
- Figurines – ceramic figurines, which were used in religious rituals, have been found at Great Courland Bay, while modelled figurine has been found at Lovers' Retreat.
- Arrowheads made of stone, bone or fish spines and spears and bows-and-arrows have been found at various sites in Tobago.

Activity

Your teacher can organise a field trip to the Tobago Museum and the First People's Community at Santa Rosa. Before you go on the field trip, work in groups and make a list of questions to which you think you will be able to find answers at the museum and the community. Record your answers, then write a reflective piece of about 200 words about our ancestors.

Project

To the map that you have already drawn in Unit 3.1, add the names of places in Trinidad and Tobago that were named by our ancestors. Research and add others.

It is known that some Amerindian inhabitants were close to the mangrove swamps of Bon Accord in the south-west part of Tobago. Some stone artefacts found at this site suggest that Amerindians lived there in approximately 3500/3000 BC.

Other important settlements in Tobago include Golden Grove, Courland River, Friendship, and Mount Irvine all in the south-west of Tobago, which were probably inhabited in the period c.300 BC–AD 650/800.

By the time of Columbus' arrival in Tobago, the island was only inhabited by one Amerindian ethnic group – the Caribs. The map shows the location of their settlements on the island.

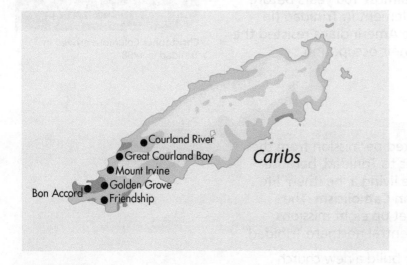

Courland River
Great Courland Bay
Mount Irvine
Golden Grove
Bon Accord
Friendship
Caribs

Activity

Watch this video about the Arawaks:

https://www.youtube.com/watch?v=g_CzfvBM5A8

Make notes while you watch the video and add it to your notes for your field trips.

Exercise

1. What evidence can be found of what life was like for the Amerindians before 1492?

2. What types of artefacts have been found at Great Courland Bay?

3. Look at the map. Why do you think many of the early settlements in Tobago were near the coast?

Key vocabulary

artefact

Indigenous people: 1492–1800

We are learning to:

- compare the experiences of the indigenous people of Tobago with those of Trinidad
- value the contribution of the indigenous people of Trinidad and Tobago.

Treatment of the Amerindians in Trinidad »

On his arrival in 1498, Columbus claimed Trinidad as a Spanish colony. His view was that Trinidad now belonged to the Spanish and that the Amerindians had no right to own the land. It took the Spanish almost 100 years before they could make a permanent settlement in Trinidad (in 1592). This was largely because the Amerindians resisted the Spanish and fought back against their occupation.

Christopher Columbus arrived in Trinidad in 1498.

Case study

The Arena Massacre

In 1686, the Spanish Governor asked permission from the King of Spain to send **missionaries** to Trinidad, because he felt that the Amerindians were living a 'heathen' life and should be converted to **Roman Catholicism**. The missionaries arrived in 1687 and set up eight missions – one of them near San Rafael, in central northern Trinidad.

In 1699, the missionaries began to build a new church at Arena, near San Rafael, using the Amerindians as the workforce. The Amerindians objected to the Roman Catholic faith and to being used as labour to build the church. The Amerindians worked slowly on the church and the missionaries threated to report them to the Governor, who was due to visit the site on 1 December 1699.

The Amerindians then attacked the priests and killed them, before ambushing the Governor and killing him and all his party – except one, who reported this back to the Spanish authorities. Soldiers were sent out to capture the escaped Amerindians, catching up with them at Cocal on the east coast and killing hundreds.

The soldiers captured 22 Amerindians, who were returned to San Jose, put on trial and sentenced to death. Today the event is seen as an act of revenge by the Spanish, who killed hundreds of people and then tortured those that they captured before sentencing them to death.

Treatment of the Amerindians in Trinidad and Tobago

The Spanish stayed in power in Trinidad until 1797, when they were pushed out by the British. By this time there were very few Amerindians left in either Trinidad or Tobago. Although the Amerindians were not treated as enslaved people – as the Africans would be later on – the Amerinidans were not treated well on either island:

- Thousands died from diseases such as influenza, measles and smallpox, brought to the islands by the Spanish.
- Others died from overwork on the Spanish cocoa estates and tobacco plantations.
- Some Amerindians were transported to work in other Spanish colonies.
- Some Amerindians fled to Venezeula or Guyana.

Soon, the numbers of Amerindians in Trinidad began to decline quite dramatically, and by 1800 they were almost extinct.

Contribution of the Amerindians

Few people today in Trinidad and Tobago are descended from the original settlers, but evidence of their presence can still be seen:

- many places in Trinidad and Tobago named by our ancestors, including: Arima, Paria, the Aripo mountains, Chaguanas, Guayaguayare and Mayaro
- plant and animal names such as carat and timite palms, tobacco, cacao, maize and manicou
- today's towns and villages are built on Amerindian settlements, such as Arima; and roads are on old trails, such as the Tumpuna Road in Arima.

Project

Your teacher will show you *The Amerindians* by filmmaker Tracey Assing. This film traces Trinidad's indigenous history and looks at the Santa Rosa Carib community. As you watch it, make notes about anything that interests you. Discuss these afterwards with your teacher.

Exercise

1. When Columbus arrived in Trinidad, who did he think now owned the island?

2. What happened in 1685, and why?

3. Outline the events of 1 December 1699.

4. How is the Arena Massacre seen today?

5. Why did it take so long for the Spanish to establish a permanent settlement in Trinidad?

6. Explain briefly why the Amerindian population declined in both Trinidad and Tobago.

Key vocabulary

missionaries

Roman Catholicism

The European presence in Tobago

We are learning to:

- analyse the impact of the early European presence on Tobago's development; Dutch, Spanish, Courlander, French, British
- identify present-day features which indicate the European presence in Tobago
- define and apply relevant terms: ward.

'Changing hands'

As we have already learned, several colonial powers fought for the control of Tobago until it finally became a British Crown Colony in 1876 (see the timeline opposite).

The Spanish had been the first to become aware of the existence of Trinidad and Tobago when Columbus came across the islands in 1498. He named Trinidad 'La Trinity.'

Some Spanish settlers came to live on La Trinity, but the Spanish did not show much interest in either La Trinity or Tobago. After that, various other European powers laid claim to Tobago at different times (see timeline).

Impact of the early European presence colonialism

The Assembly of Tobago provided some degree of self-government, although only a small percentage of the population could vote for the elected deputies. Out of every 100 people who lived on the island, 94 were enslaved African people, who had been brought to the island to work on the plantations.

In 1793, Tobago was captured by the British. The running of the island as given over to the British Crown. All male inhabitants had to take an **oath of allegiance** to the British Crown, and those who did not were regarded as prisoners of war. In 1802, Tobago was given back to the French, only to be recaptured by British again the following year. In 1833, Tobago became part of the Windward Islands.

Tobago was a prosperous island as a result of the tobacco plantations and later the sugar and cotton plantations. Enslaved people were brought from Africa to work on the plantations. Tobago traded with Guyana and Barbados more than with Trinidad.

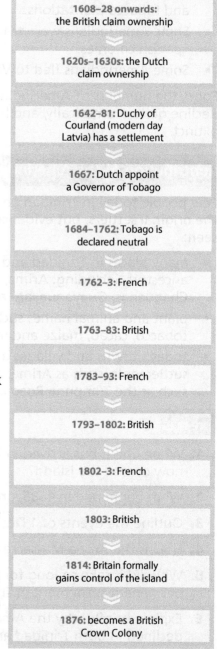

1608–28 onwards: the British claim ownership

1620s–1630s: the Dutch claim ownership

1642–81: Duchy of Courland (modern day Latvia) has a settlement

1667: Dutch appoint a Governor of Tobago

1684–1762: Tobago is declared neutral

1762–3: French

1763–83: British

1783–93: French

1793–1802: British

1802–3: French

1803: British

1814: Britain formally gains control of the island

1876: becomes a British Crown Colony

When the island became a British **Crown Colony** in 1876, it was ruled by a Governor appointed by the British Crown and a council appointed by the Governor. The island was divided into parishes for the purposes of administration. In 1899, a series of economic and political problems – it was decided that Tobago could no longer be a separate colony. It then became a **ward** (a division) of Trinidad.

Since then, Tobago and Trinidad have been one nation, becoming an independent state in 1962 and the Republic of Trinidad and Tobago in 1976.

The Arnos Vale Waterwheel in Tobago.

Present-day features

One legacy of the European presence in Tobago's early history is the number of place names with Dutch, Spanish, French and British origin:

- **Dutch:** Courland Bay, Luggarts Bay (later renamed Minister Bay by the British)
- **Spanish:** Tobago, Cape Gracias-a-Dios, Pedro Point
- **French:** Charlotteville, Bacolet
- **British:** Arnos Vale, Calder Hall.

Historical landmarks include:

- Arnos Vale waterwheel – built in 1857, this was part of a 19th century British sugar mill.
- Fort King George – built by the British in 1777, this was later occupied by French troops; visitors can still see the ruins of the fort, including the officers' mess, lighthouse and bell tower.

Exercise

1. Name the European countries that claimed Tobago.
2. What was the name that Columbus gave Trinidad?
3. Why do you think European powers were attracted to Tobago?
4. When did Tobago become a British Crown Colony?

Did you know...?

One of the reasons countries fought over Tobago was because the island provided natural safe harbours.

Research

Using the internet, research European place names in Tobago. Find pictures of each settlement as they look today, and add them to your research.

Key vocabulary

oath of allegiance

ward

Economics and politics in Tobago: 1800s

We are learning to:

- compare the economic and political experiences of the people of Tobago with that of Trinidad in the 1800s
- present using various media our understanding of the social, economic and political development of Tobago.

British colonial period in Tobago

During the 1800s, Trinidad was ruled by a single colonial power (the British) but, as we have seen, in the same period Tobago was ruled by a number of different colonial powers. Tobago finally became a British colony in 1876, although they had been under British rule since 1814.

When the British took Tobago from the French in 1783, a number of sugar plantations that used enslaved African people were set up. This was a prosperous period for the plantation owners, but when the slave trade was brought to an end in 1807 the loss of cheap labour meant that profits were much smaller. The economy of Tobago quickly began to decline.

In the first half of the 19th century, sugar was the main industry in Trinidad.

Economic development in Trinidad, 1800s

In the first half of the 19th century, sugar was the main industry in Trinidad. After emancipation in 1838, many formerly enslaved people moved away from the plantations. A labour shortage led to the indentureship of immigrants, which helped the sugar industry to remain prosperous.

However, by the 1880s, the sugar industry in Trinidad was also in decline. This was partly due to competition from countries such as Cuba, but also because production costs in Trinidad had started to increase. This resulted in exports costing more. Countries such as America began to buy the cheaper Cuban sugar, which had a big impact on Trinidad's ability to export at cost-effective prices.

Exercise

1. What was the main industry in Tobago in the late 1800s?

2. Why did the sugar industry continue to prosper in Trinidad after emancipation?

3. Give reasons for the decline of the sugar industry in Trinidad in the late 1800s.

Tobago House of Assembly ▶▶▶

In 1768, the first Tobago **House of Assembly** met in Georgetown, which is now called Studley Park. Georgetown was the capital of the island at that time. Members of the Assembly were elected, but only white men who owned land or houses could hold a seat. These were the plantation owners.

Following emancipation, in order to be eligible to vote you needed to own property or have a large income. Formerly enslaved people had neither, so were unable to take part in the election. In 1857, only 102 people out of a population of 15 000 (0.7%) were allowed to vote.

In 1876, this representative government was abolished by the British administration. Tobago was granted the same type of government as Trinidad and became a British Crown Colony.

Trinidad – Crown Colony government ▶

In 1802, Trinidad was officially made a British Crown Colony. The island was ruled by a Governor, who represented the British Crown in London.

At this point the island was still run under old Spanish laws, which the British Crown did not always favour. Therefore, in 1831, a **Legislative Council** was formed to run the island.

The new laws were made to favour the estate owners and Trinidadians were not allowed to vote. Tax laws also seemed to favour the estate owners, with the result that the cost of food for the average Trinidadian increased.

Despite all of this, by the 1880s the Trinidad's economy was doing much better than that of Tobago.

Activity

Imagine that you worked on a sugar plantation in Trinidad in 1850. In what ways would your life be different from, or similar to, someone who worked on a sugar plantation in Tobago. Examine your working and living conditions and political rights.

Exercise

4. Where and when did the Tobago Assembly first meet?

5. Who could be elected to the first Assembly, and why?

6. What were the requirements that allowed you to vote after emancipation in Tobago?

7. Name the body that ran Trinidad from 1831.

8. True or false? The new laws brought in by the Legislative Council in Trinidad favoured ordinary Trinidadians.

Key vocabulary

House of Assembly

Legislative Council

Politics and religion in Tobago: 1800s

We are learning to:

- compare the economic and political experiences of the people of Tobago with that of Trinidad in the 1800s
- present using various media our understanding of the social, economic and political development of Tobago: educational and religious developments.

Tobago's union with Trinidad

By the 1880s, Tobago's economy was in crisis. Most of the estates were no longer producing sugar and the government had little money to spend on improving things because tax revenues were so small. The British did not want to send money to support the islands' economy.

The British saw that Trinidad's economy was in much better shape than Tobago's. They thought that a solution would be to **annex** Tobago to Trinidad, to save costs. The factors which led to this **annexation** included:

- labour shortages and the weakening of the income from plantations, due to the emancipation of enslaved people
- the collapse of the sugar industry in general
- the destruction caused by a hurricane in 1847
- labour unrest and strikes in 1876 that ended in riots.

On 1 January 1889, Tobago was annexed to Trinidad and the two islands were ruled as one state. Tobago lost its local assembly and instead it was administered by a Commissioner, appointed by the **Governor** of Trinidad. Initially Tobago retained its right to set tax levels. The British removed this right in 1899 and integrated the tax system across both islands.

Coat of arms of Trinidad and Tobago.

Discussion

In groups, discuss the social, economic and political changes in Trinidad and Tobago in the 1800s. Do you think Trinidad and Tobago were better places to live by 1899 than they had been in 1800? Why, or why not?

Exercise

1. Explain in your own words why Tobago's economy was in crisis by the 1880s.
2. What was the British solution to Tobago's economic problems?
3. When was Tobago annexed to Trinidad?
4. In groups, discuss whether you agree with the British solution: annexing Tobago to Trinidad. Do you feel it was fair to Trinidad to support Tobago, rather than for the British to continue supporting both islands?

Each of the various groups of inhabitants and immigrants to Trinidad and Tobago and the wider Caribbean have contributed to our wide variety of religious practices – from the original Amerindians, to the Spanish, French, Dutch and British. For example:

Queen's Royal College is the oldest secondary school in Trinidad and Tobago.

- **Roman Catholicism** – introduced to the Caribbean region by the Spanish and French
- **Protestant** denominations, such as **Anglicanism**, **Methodism** and **Presbyterianism** – introduced by the British
- **Moravian** Protestantism – introduced by German missionaries in the 18th century to the Eastern West Indies, including Trinidad and Tobago
- **Hinduism** and **Islam** – introduced by the indentured Indians.

By the 1800s, Tobago was almost an entirely Protestant island, made up of Anglican, Methodist and Moravian churches. These churches also provided schooling for the island.

Because of the influence of the French and Spanish, in Trinidad Roman Catholicism was the most prominent religion. There were some Protestant churches in Trinidad, mainly as a result of the British estate owners and government officials, who were Anglicans. By the end of the 1800s in Trinidad, almost all the main denominations had set up schools – Catholic, Anglican, Methodist and Moravian.

The growth of schools provided by the different **denominations** in both Trinidad and Tobago was influenced by the churches' desire to teach their own religious practices. Sometimes, rival schools would be set up in villages, so that one church could try and draw people away from other religions.

Key vocabulary

annex/annexation

governor

Protestant

Anglicanism

Methodism

Presbyterianism

Moravian

Hinduism

Islam

denomination

Exercise

5. Draw a mind map or a graphic organiser of the religions in Trinidad and Tobago in the 1800s, also showing which country they come from.

6. Which religion dominated Tobago in the 1800s?

7. Who introduced Hinduism and Islam to Trinidad and Tobago in the second part of the 19th century?

8. Explain the growth of the number of schools by the end of the 19th century.

Economic systems in Trinidad and Tobago: the sugar industry (1)

We are learning to:

- discuss the sugar industry, apprenticeship, peasantry and the metayage system.

Sugar and our heritage

Dutch settlers planted sugar cane in 1630 in Trinidad. In 1783, a French sugar planter called Philippe Roume de St Laurent arrived with other settlers and enslaved people. Although the French settlers planted more cane in the 1780s, it was the arrival of the British in 1797 that turned the island into a large-scale sugar colony.

The plantation labourers were enslaved African people, until the abolition of **slavery** in 1834. The plantation owners then introduced an **apprenticeship** system.

Apprenticeships and peasant farming

Apprenticeships were for formerly enslaved people who had to serve their former owners free of charge for 40.5 hours a week for 4 to 6 years. They were paid for any extra hours that they worked. The system caused a lot of conflict, and finally – on 1 August 1838 – all enslaved people in the British West Indies were given full **emancipation**.

An enslaved woman hoeing sugar plants.

After the abolition of slavery (between 1845 and 1917), the British brought indentured labourers from China, India and Madeira.

Enslaved people who had been set free started up their own small businesses and small farms in order to feed themselves and support their families. This was the beginning of **peasant farming** in Trinidad and Tobago. Peasant farmers grew foods such as yams, cassava, corn, coconuts, bananas, peas, sugar, cocoa and coffee and reared livestock, such as poultry.

Exercise

1. Where did the first sugar farmers come from?
2. Which event turned the sugar industry into a large-scale industry?
3. Define the terms apprenticeship and peasant farming.

Case study

The metayage system

Emancipation in 1834 did not hit Tobago nearly as hard as Trinidad. Tobago had no free Crown lands for formerly enslaved people to squat upon, so those who did not emigrate had no alternative but to continue working for the planters.

In order to keep sugar estates going, the **metayage system**, which was a form of sharecropping, developed. Under the system, the metayer (sharecropper) occupied a piece of land on which he or she planted cane.

At harvest time, the estate owner supplied carts which drew cut canes to the mill, where they were processed into rum and sugar of which the metayer received a percentage. In addition, the metayer was often allowed permission to build a cottage on the estate and provision grounds.

'Such was the depression at that time, that had not the labourer been induced to work for a share of the produce, the estates, for want of means to pay in money for labour, must have gone out of cultivation.'

The rise and fall of sugar ▶▶▶

In 1937, there were two important events in the history of the sugar industry: the formation of a sugar workers' union and the establishment of Caroni, a sugar company that brought together many smaller sugar companies under the ownership of British company Tate & Lyle.

In 1975, the government of Trinidad bought out Caroni and all the other sugar companies, forming Caroni (1975) Limited but, due to the decline in the sugar industry, the state closed it down in 2003 (see 3.8).

(see 3.8)

Research

Using the internet, and working in groups, research what life was like for people under the metayage system. See if you can find any evidence of it being used in your community or area. Discuss whether you think it was a good or bad system for those who farmed this way.

Did you know...?

Sugar was so important that it was known as King Sugar.

Key vocabulary

slavery

apprenticeship

emancipation

peasant farming

metayage system

Exercise

4. Explain in your own words the term metayage.

5. Which two events took place that contributed to the rise of sugar in the 20th century?

6. What do you understand from the term King Sugar?

Economic systems in Trinidad and Tobago: the sugar industry (2)

We are learning to:

- discuss the problems in the sugar industry, agricultural diversification and the decline of the sugar industry.

Problems in the sugar industry 》

For about 200 years – between the mid-1700s and mid-1900s – Trinidad and Tobago received most of its revenue from the production of sugar. However, the sugar industry was in decline all the way up to the 1970s. There were several reasons for this:

Workers at a coffee plantation, Port of Spain, Trinidad, around 1890.

- Following emancipation in 1838, the formerly enslaved people on the islands preferred to use land for other types of farming: livestock; ground crops, including dasheen, yam and cassava; vegetables, such as corn and peas; fruits, like cocoa, bananas and oranges.

- Similarly, many East Indians had land of their own following the end of indentureship. Like the formerly enslaved people, they preferred to grow other crops, including crops from India such as rice.

- By the 1930s, the sugar industry in Trinidad and Tobago was facing competition from other industries. Both Cuban sugar and European beet sugar were much cheaper to produce, and plantations in Trinidad and Tobago could not compete.

1. In your own words, outline some of the problems the sugar industry in Trinidad and Tobago faced.

2. Trinidad and Tobago faced competition from the sugar industries in which of the following?

    a) Jamaica

    b) Cuba and Europe

    c) Europe and India.

Agricultural diversification

In 1975, many sugar estates were closing down or laying off workers. So, the government aimed to save jobs by buying all the sugar companies, forming Caroni (1975) Limited, and diversifying into other types of farming:

- Dairy farming – at Mon Jaloux farm, sheep and cattle farming for production of meat and milk.
- Buffalypso – a new breed of cattle, developed by Caroni, which was very low in fat. At La Gloria and Mora Valley, buffalypso were reared for production of beef.
- Rice – at Guayamare, more than 6 square km of land were turned into rice paddies.
- Coffee and citrus – all over the islands, thousands of hectares of land became used for coffee beans and citrus fruits such as oranges.
- Other fruits – some sugar farms were converted to other crops, including cassava, pigeon peas and plantain, as well as tropical fruits like pineapple, pawpaw and passion fruit.

Sugar cane cutting.

Why did Caroni need to diversify?

The reasons for diversification included:

- The cost of production was too high in comparison to other countries. Foreign countries (for example, Cuba) could produce sugar more cheaply.
- Caroni was making a loss.
- Caroni was relying on finance borrowed from the government.
- The company was unable to pay its suppliers.
- The government wanted to create linkages for a range of agricultural products.
- Sugar cane produced in Trinidad and Tobago has a lower yield (how much cane is needed to produce 1 tonne of sugar) than that from other countries.

Despite this, the government closed Caroni (1975) Limited in 2003.

Discussion

If the government had not bought the sugar farms and formed Caroni (1975) Ltd what do you think would have happened?

Activity

Use the internet to carry out research on the closure of Caroni (1975) Limited. Present a one-minute news report summarising what you have discovered.

Exercise

3. List the new products that Trinidad and Tobago started producing once Caroni (1975) Limited started agricultural diversification.

4. Draw a graphic organiser showing the reasons why the company needed to diversify.

Key vocabulary

diversify

Key figures who fought social injustice

We are learning to:

- examine the role played by key figures/significant individuals during the period
- appreciate the motivations of key figures during the period.

The 1930s saw a big change for the working classes in Trinidad and Tobago. From the early 20th century, the sugar industry had been in decline and, although the new oil industry in Trinidad was profitable, wages for the working class were low and the oil companies exploited the workers.

Workers did not have **political suffrage**. In order to vote, they either had to have a high income or own property. Very few workers qualified, so in a period of high unemployment and low wages there was a lot of social unrest. During this period, there emerged some important figures in the history of Trinidad of Tobago who fought social injustice.

Bishop Anstey high school for girls, Port of Spain, Trinidad 1961.

Profile

James Biggart (1877–1932)

- The first black elected Member of the Trinidad and Tobago Legislative Council (1925–32).
- The first black pharmacist in Tobago.
- In 1909, raised social issues in Tobago with the Governor of the island, including the need of a high school for girls and boys and self-governance.
- A member of the committee that helped establish the first public library in Scarborough, Tobago.
- Part of the group that helped to raise funds to build the Bishop Anstey High School in Port of Spain in 1925. The aim of the school was to ensure that girls had the same educational opportunities as boys, regardless of their background.
- Posthumously awarded the Tobago Medal of Honour in 2011, the highest mark of distinction Tobago could award one of its citizens.

Activity

Role-play an event in the life of either James Biggart, A.P.T. James or A.N.R. Robinson.

Did you know...?

A.N.R. Robinson, James Biggart and A.P.T. James were all awarded the Tobago Medal of Honour at the same ceremony in 2011. Biggart and James were awarded their awards posthumously.

Exercise

1. In the early 20th century, what did you need to have to be allowed to vote? Do you think this was fair?
2. What contribution did James Biggart make to Trinidad and Tobago?

Profile

A.N.R. Robinson (1926–2014)

- The only person in the history of Trinidad and Tobago to have held three of the highest public offices – the first chairman of the Tobago House of Assembly (1980), Prime Minister of Trinidad and Tobago (1986–91) and President of the Republic of Trinidad and Tobago (1997–2003).
- In 1961, elected to the Parliament of Trinidad and Tobago as an MP for Tobago.
- In 1962, appointed as the nation's first Minister of Finance and responsible for reforming the economic policies of the nation after independence had been awarded in 1962.
- Established the Democratic Action Congress party in 1971 and won a seat in the 1976 general election.
- A lifetime advocate for democracy, unity and human rights.
- The founding father of the United Nations International Criminal Court (ICC).
- Awarded the Tobago Medal of Honour in 2011.

Profile

A.P.T. James (1907–62)

- A politician who supported Tobago being independent of Trinidad.
- Argued that social and economic changes were taking a long time in Tobago, because central government was in Trinidad and not in Tobago.
- Won a parliamentary seat representing Tobago in the 1946 general election.
- Campaigned for greater representation for Tobago and self-government, and helped people in Tobago to purchase land or pay their land rents when they were unable to do so.
- Was posthumously awarded the Tobago Medal of Honour in 2011, the highest mark of distinction Tobago could award one of its citizens.

Exercise

3. What contributions did A.N.R. Robinson and A.P.T. James make to Trinidad and Tobago?

4. Who is the only person in the history of Trinidad and Tobago to have held three of the highest public offices?

5. Create a timeline of all the key events in the lives of A.N.R. Robinson, James Biggart and A.P.T. James.

Key vocabulary

political suffrage

Tobago House of Assembly

We are learning to:

- outline issues related to the functioning of the THA: structure and function of the modern THA.

Tobago House of Assembly: 1980 to present day

During the 1970s, Robinson campaigned to reintroduce the House of Assembly, so Tobago could take control of its own local affairs. In 1980, the Tobago House of Assembly (THA) was established to manage matters affecting the island of Tobago. It is part of the local government of Trinidad and Tobago.

The THA originally existed in the period 1768–1874, before Trinidad and Tobago became one nation. Back then, the THA was run by the ruling Crown Colony, and election to the House was almost impossible for ordinary workers: you had to be a white Christian male, be older than 21 and own at least 40 000 square metres of land.

Functions of the THA

The THA manages local and central government responsibilities, and is able to take certain decisions that affect the island. Matters of national security, foreign affairs, civil aviation, immigration and legal affairs are still under the control of the national government. The Assembly has to take the national policies of government into consideration when carrying out its functions.

Did you know...?

In the 1961 general election, A.N.R. Robinson defeated A.P.T. James to win the East Tobago seat.

Exercise

1. In which year was the THA established for the second time?

2. Why was the THA established?

3. Why was election to the previous THA almost impossible for ordinary workers?

Research

Research the current Assembly Members of the THA. Then draw your own version of the THA's structure, adding where in the THA the current Assembly Members sit.

Some of the Assembly's functions are to:

- collect certain taxes and pay expenses
- promote and regulate tourism
- administer state lands including parks
- administer museums, historical sites and buildings
- promote and support sports, culture and the arts.

The structure of the THA >>>

In 1980, after the THA was formed, it was split into seven divisions, each division representing an area of government. Today, there are 10 such divisions, which are overseen by two main branches: the **Legislative Arm** and the **Executive Arm**.

Look at the diagram showing the structure of the House of Assembly:

Key vocabulary

Legislative Arm

Executive Arm

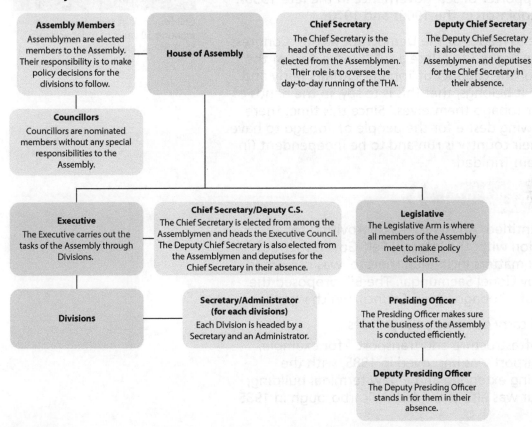

Assembly Members
Assemblymen are elected members to the Assembly. Their responsibility is to make policy decisions for the divisions to follow.

House of Assembly

Chief Secretary
The Chief Secretary is the head of the executive and is elected from the Assemblymen. Their role is to oversee the day-to-day running of the THA.

Deputy Chief Secretary
The Deputy Chief Secretary is also elected from the Assemblymen and deputises for the Chief Secretary in their absence.

Councillors
Councillors are nominated members without any special responsibilities to the Assembly.

Executive
The Executive carries out the tasks of the Assembly through Divisions.

Chief Secretary/Deputy C.S.
The Chief Secretary is elected from among the Assemblymen and heads the Executive Council. The Deputy Chief Secretary is also elected from the Assemblymen and deputises for the Chief Secretary in their absence.

Legislative
The Legislative Arm is where all members of the Assembly meet to make policy decisions.

Divisions

Secretary/Administrator (for each divisions)
Each Division is headed by a Secretary and an Administrator.

Presiding Officer
The Presiding Officer makes sure that the business of the Assembly is conducted efficiently.

Deputy Presiding Officer
The Deputy Presiding Officer stands in for them in their absence.

Exercise

4. Look at the diagram showing the structure of the THA.

   Then answer these questions.

   a) What is the purpose of the Legislative Arm of the THA?
   b) What is the role of the Assemblymen and Chief Executive?
   c) In which part of the THA are the Divisions and the Presiding Officer?

Tobago House of Assembly (2)

We are learning to:

- outline issues related to the functioning of the THA: quest for self-government: finance.

The quest for self-government for Tobago

We have seen how in the late 19th century Tobago became a ward of Trinidad. Since then, Tobago and Trinidad have been one nation, becoming an independent state in 1962 and then the Republic of Trinidad and Tobago in 1976. A.P.T. James was a supporter of self-governance in the late 1950s, as was A.N.R. Robinson in the 1960s and 1970s.

During his time as leader of the Democratic Action Congress (DAC), Robinson argued to 'place a substantial part of the responsibility for the conduct of Tobago's affairs fairly and squarely where it belongs; that this is to say, in the hands of the residents of Tobago themselves.' Since this time, there has been a growing desire for the people of Tobago to have a say in how their country is run and to be independent (in this respect) from Trinidad.

Children look at the decorations marking 50 years of independence for Trinidad and Tobago.

The Seemungal Bill (1979)

In 1979, a Bill entitled 'An Act to make provision for, and in connection with, the Internal Self-Government of Tobago, and all matters incidental thereto' was presented to Parliament by Lionel Seemungal. The Bill proposed the establishment of a Tobago Island Council, which would:

- create and carry out economic policies
- improve infrastructure and transport – for example, Tobago's airport was improved in 1985, with the runway being extended and a new terminal building; the harbour was also extended in Scarborough in 1985
- raise taxes.

The Seemungal Bill was rejected by the government, but this did lead to the Tobago House of Assembly Act (1980), which led to the formation of the Tobago House of Assembly.

Exercise

1. Explain the purpose of the Seemungal Bill. Use your own words.

2. What happened as a result of the Seemungal Bill?

However, as we have seen, Tobago was still a ward of Trinidad and was not considered wholly independent.

Tobago House of Assembly Act, 1996 ›››

In 1996, the Tobago House of Assembly Act enabled Tobago to manage aspects of its affairs, including sports and culture, fishing, state lands, food production and agriculture, tourism and health services. However, other issues – such as national security, immigration, foreign affairs and judiciary and legal affairs – remained with Trinidad.

The Tobago House of Assembly currently has a Finance and the Economy division.

Since 1996, there has been a growing opinion amongst the people of Tobago that they should be allowed more self-government, which will enable the island to manage its economic, social and cultural development more effectively. For example:

- 2005 – the THA called on the government to reform the constitution according to the will of the Tobago people.
- 2006 – an amendment to the constitution was rejected, as there had been no public consultation on what the relationship should be between Trinidad and Tobago if self-governance was achieved.
- 2020 – The Constitution Amendment (Tobago self-government) Bill was introduced by Prime Minister Keith Rowley. Its provisions include `the right of the people of Tobago to determine their political status and freely pursue their economic, social and cultural development'.
- 2021 – the bill was amended and is currently being debated. The issue of secession also forms part of the debate.

Finance ››

The Tobago House of Assembly currently has a Finance and the Economy division which oversees Tobago's financial requirements. This includes:

- distributing funds
- collecting tax revenue and revenue from trade
- an internal audit department, which reviews the running of the divisions of the THA
- an enterprise department whose role is to develop business growth.

Project

Create a short report on the history of Tobago's quest for self-governance. Write 150–200 words. Explain why Tobago wanted self-governance, the attempts to achieve this and the issues behind it. To illustrate your report, add photos found on the internet or in magazines.

Key vocabulary

secession

Exercise

3. What affairs of the nation did Tobago gain control of in 1996?

4. Why do you think the 1996 Act was not satisfactory for Tobago?

5. Explain the financial aspect of its economy currently overseen by the Tobago House of Assembly.

Challenges to the social order

We are learning to:

- define and apply relevant terms and concepts: adult suffrage, democracy
- explain the contribution of key figures and groups in the fields of trade unionism and social activism to Trinidad and Tobago 1900–70.

Adult suffrage

The 1920s and 1930s saw a big change in the expectations of working people – not only in Trinidad and Tobago, but all over the Caribbean and other parts of the world. Workers wanted better working conditions, respect and the freedom to protest if necessary.

Workers forced the government to take notice of them and to recognise them. This was the beginnings of **social activism** and **social justice**, which led to the development of trade unions and political parties.

Workers digging and transporting natural deposits of asphalt at Pitch Lake, La Brea, Trinidad, c. 1935.

Constitutional reform began in 1922, when the Wood Commission allowed people in Trinidad and Tobago the vote. However, this was a limited franchise, because to be able to vote men had to be over the age of 21 and women over 31, and they had to own property over a certain value or have a high income. This small start was the beginning of representative government and **democracy** in the state.

After further social unrest in the 1930s, in 1939 the Moyne Commission recommended the lowering of voting qualifications. In 1945, all citizens over the age of 21 were given the right to vote. **Adult suffrage** had been achieved, which was another step on the road to self-government for Trinidad and Tobago. The first elections in which all adults were allowed to vote took place on 1 July 1946.

Discussion

At present you have to be 18 years old to vote in Trinidad and Tobago. Do you think the present voting age is appropriate? Give reasons for your answer.

Exercise

1. **a)** Who was eligible to vote for the Legislative Council in 1922?

   b) Do you think this was a fair system? Give a reason for your answer.

2. What did the Moyne Commission recommend?

3. What was so important about the 1946 elections?

The first political party in Trinidad and Tobago was registered in 1934. This was the Trinidad Labour Party (TLP), and was led by A.A. Cipriani.

In 1936, the Trinidad Citizens League under the leadership of Adrian 'Cola' Rienzi and T.U.B. Butler was registered. As adults achieved full suffrage, more and more political parties were established to represent all the different interests in Trinidad and Tobago.

There was a Socialist Party and a West Indian National Party, as well as a United Front party. In 1950, the People's National Movement (PNM) was formed. The PNM was to dominate politics in Trinidad and Tobago in the years leading up to independence. This party was led by Dr Eric Williams.

In 1950, there were further constitutional reforms that made the state **semi-autonomous**. The number of members of the Legislative Council was increased to 24. And with this change came the start of majority party politics. Whichever party won the most seats on the Council controlled the Council. Additional political parties continued to be established.

People's National Movement Party became the **majority** or **ruling party** after the 1956 elections.

However, Trinidad and Tobago was still not yet self-governing. The Governor was still appointed by the British government and some of the Council members were still appointed by the Governor. But political stability gave leaders from different parties the confidence to cooperate and to push ahead with plans for independence.

Supporters of the People's National Movement (PNM).

Research

Work in pairs and do your own research about one of the political parties that emerged in the 1950s. Find out:

- who led the party
- what the party stood for
- how well they did in elections
- whether the party still exists.

Exercise

4. Name two political parties that were formed in Trinidad and Tobago before 1950.

5. Name the party that was formed in 1950 and give the name of its leader.

6. Define the terms social activism, social justice and adult suffrage.

7. Create a timeline to summarise the process to achieve adult suffrage and the emergence of political parties in Trinidad and Tobago in the 20th century.

Key vocabulary

social activism

social justice

democracy

adult suffrage

semi-autonomous

majority/ruling party

Key figures in trade unionism

We are learning to:

- explain the contribution of key figures and groups in the fields of trade unionism and social activism to Trinidad and Tobago 1900–70
- use primary and secondary sources to research the origins of the early trade unions in the early 20th century.

Tubal Uriah 'Buzz' Butler

T.U.B. Butler was one of the most well-known political figures in Trinidad in the early 20th century. From an early age, Butler had strong principles to fight for democracy and to end injustice. He fought in World War I and in the early 1920s worked in the Trinidad oilfields. In response to the social unrest of the 1930s, he founded the Trinidad Labour Party (TLP) with A.A. Cipriani in 1934.

In 1935, Butler organised a 'hunger march' from the Apex oilfields in Fyzabad to the Governor's residence in Port of Spain. Butler gave a speech on the march, which directly addressed the problems faced by oilfield workers, including: bad labour contracts, job insecurity, poor wages and incentives, and lack of transport for the workers to and from the work sites.

T.U.B. Butler worked in the oilfields in Trinidad.

Cipriani disagreed with Butler's more aggressive methods of bringing these issues to people's attention. Therefore, in 1936 Butler left the TLP and formed his own party – the Trinidad Citizens League (TCL) – with Adrian 'Cola' Rienzi. In 1937, he called a strike at Trinidad Leaseholds Limited oilfields. The strike spread to other oilfields. At one rally, there were riots. Two police officers were killed and oil wells were set on fire. Butler was imprisoned for causing a riot.

When he was released in 1945, he formed the Butler Party, whose aim was to unite people of East Indian and African descent in Trinidad and Tobago. His party won seats in the 1951 election and he continued to take an active part in the politics of Trinidad and Tobago until his death in 1977.

Activity

Your teacher could organise a field trip to the Oilfields Workers' Trade Union (OWTU) headquarters in San Fernando.

Activity

Your teacher will show you documentaries about the riots in the 1930s and the commemoration of Labour Day. Watch the videos, then create a short report about one of the events. Use pictures from the internet.

Exercise

1. What political party did Butler form in 1934?

2. What were the reasons that Butler organised the 'hunger march' in 1935?

3. In your own words, explain what happened in 1937, and the consequences.

Profile

Adrian 'Cola' Rienzi (1905–72)

- Trade unionist, lawyer and politician, whose aim was to make Trinidad a better place for working people.
- Formed the Trinidad Citizens League (TCL) with TUB Butler in 1936.
- Later helped to form the Oilfields Workers' Trade Union (OWTU) in 1937.
- The first president of the Trinidad and Tobago Trade Union Council (1938–44).
- Member of the Legislative Council (1937–44).
- Achievements included: helping Indian immigrants gain employment in the public sector, and the establishment of non-Christian schools.

A stamp printed in Trinidad and Tobago from the Labour Day issue shows labour leaders Adrian 'Cola' Rienzi and C.T.W.E. Worrell, circa 1985.

Profile

George Weekes (1921–95)

- Trade unionist and activist.
- Joined the OWTU in 1950 and President General of the OWTU, 1962–87.
- Aligned himself and his followers with the Black Power Movement of 1970; arrested during one of the marches.
- Achievements included: saving the jobs of BP workers in 1963, arguing the case that the oil industry should be nationalised, and introducing a popular movement of **social militancy** into Trinidad and Tobago, and the Caribbean.

Other important labour activists in this period include Elma Francois (1897–1944), a trade unionist who co-founded the Negro Welfare Cultural and Social Association (NWCSA), whose aim was to unite workers together to fight for better conditions. She took part in T.U.B. Butler's 'hunger' march in 1935, and in June 1937, together with Butler and others, led the historic general strike. She was the first woman in Trinidad to be arrested in 1938 and tried for sedition. The jury found her not guilty.

Research

Work in groups. Using the internet, research the route of the 'hunger march' in 1935.

Did you know...?

Labour Day is celebrated on 19 June every year in Trinidad and Tobago. This holiday commemorates the anniversary of the 1937 Butler labour riots.

Exercise

4. What contributions did Adrian Rienzi and George Weekes make to Trinidad and Tobago?

5. What organisation did Elma Francois found?

Key vocabulary

social militancy

Origins of trade unions

We are learning to:

- use primary and secondary sources to research the origins of the trade unions in the early 20th century
- explain the contribution of key figures and groups in the fields of trade unionism and social activism to Trinidad and Tobago 1900–70.

Trinidad Working Men's Association (TWA) ❯❯

The origins of the TWA go back to 1894, when the Working Men's Association (WMA) was formed to represent skilled workers of African descent who were masons, carpenters, railway workers and store clerks. The association was renamed the Trinidad Working Men's Association (TWA) in 1906, and in 1923 A.A. Cipriani was appointed its president.

The aims of the TWA were to campaign for:

- improvements to workers' wages
- better working conditions
- shorter working hours
- paid holidays and sick leave
- compensation for any injuries gained while at work.

The TWA quickly became one of the most popular labour organisations in Trinidad. This was partly due to the charismatic appeal of Cipriani, but also because the TWA remained firmly committed to the fight for workers' rights. Some estimates put the number of members in the TWA at 70 000 by 1933. Branches also opened in Tobago.

The TWA was also a political party. In 1925, Cipriani was elected to the Legislative Council and through this position he tried to help change the laws in the workers' favour. The TWA was renamed the Trinidad Labour Party in 1934 when the trade union decided to enter politics.

Statue of Captain Cipriani in downtown Port of Spain, Trinidad.

Exercise

1. In which year was the Trinidad Working Men's Association founded?

2. Which workers did the TWA have as its members?

3. What were the aims of the TWA?

4. Who became the President of the TWA in 1936?

5. Why was the TWA also considered to be a political party?

The Oilfield Workers' Trade Union (OWTU) was founded in 1937, when T.U.B. Butler called a strike at Trinidad Leaseholds Limited oilfields to protest about working conditions. The strike spread to other oilfields and then into other workers in the industry, such as dock workers, sugar workers and railway workers.

When the strike was over on 2 July, the OWTU was formed. Its first meeting took place on 15 July 1937 and it was formally registered as a union on 15 September that year.

The aim of the OWTU was to protect the rights of its members (the oil workers), as well the wider working class and the nation of Trinidad and Tobago.

Adrian 'Cola' Rienzi was the OWTU's first president general. Rienzi's approach was to adopt 'an organised means of **collective bargaining** through which the claims or grievances of the workpeople could have found ample means of expression.'

Today, the OWTU is one of the largest and most powerful trade unions in Trinidad and Tobago and represents more than 11 000 oilfield workers.

The labour movements of the 1920s and 1930s are all expressions of our nation's struggle for social justice and equality. As we have seen, examples in this period include:

- constitutional reform and adult suffrage
- the emergence of political parties and trade unions
- the 'hunger march' of 1935 and general strike of 1937.

Exercise

6. In what year was the OWTU founded?

7. What was the aim of the OWTU?

8. Who became the President of the OWTU?

9. Why do you think the OWTU was formed after the general strike in 1937 and not beforehand?

10. In your own words, explain the term collective bargaining.

Activity

Using this link http://archive.owtu.org/content/about-us research the history of the OWTU. Then, in your own words, write a short report on the history of the OWTU from 1937. Include key events and milestones, the people involved and the aims of the OWTU when it was founded. Add any photos that you can find.

Project

Look back on Units 3.13–3.15. Imagine you are a mason, carpenter, railway worker, store clerk or oil worker working in Trinidad and Tobago in the 1920s and 1930s. In groups, role-play why you may be unhappy about your work. Create some slogans that could be used as protest banners about your work.

Activity

Using a graphic organiser – such as a mind map or timeline – compile key events in the history of the TWA and OWTU in the period 1894–1937.

Key vocabulary

collective bargaining

Challenges to the social order (2)

We are learning to:

- explain the contribution of key figures and groups in the fields of trade unionism and social activism to Trinidad and Tobago 1900–70
- value the ideals of social justice, volunteerism.

Social workers

As well as the struggles for workers' rights by the trade unions, and the emerging political parties, during the 1920s and 1930s there were also a number of individuals in Trinidad and Tobago who cared about those less fortunate in society.

Audrey Jeffers (1898–1968) was a social worker who did a lot of work in Trinidad to help the underprivileged and homeless. In the early 1920s, the economy was in steady decline, resulting in high unemployment, low wages, widespread poverty and slum living.

In 1920, Jeffers started a junior school in her home and in 1921 formed the Coterie of Social Workers (CSW), which provided free lunches for poor school children in Port of Spain. This was known as the 'breakfast shed.' Soon, the breakfast sheds also opened in San Fernando, Arima and Siparia. The CSW went on to establish homes for the elderly, the blind, hostels for young women and day nurseries.

Audrey Jeffers

In 1936, Jeffers became the first woman to be elected to the Port of Spain City Council. Today, the legacy of her breakfast shed initiative can be seen in school meals provided by the government.

Clothil Walcott (1925–2007) was a trade union activist who campaigned about the oppression and exploitation of women in the workplace. In the early 1970s, she helped domestic workers to gain more protection under the labour laws and helped to form the National Union of Domestic Employees (NUDE).

Exercise

1. Explain Audrey Jeffers' contribution to Trinidad.
2. Name the organisation Jeffers founded in 1921, and its purpose.

An early example of the population standing up for social justice occurred in 1903 with the so-called 'water riots.' A report in 1880 found that there was a large amount of water being wasted in Port of Spain: 'In nearly every yard, and at almost every house, passersby in the street will hear the sound of water running.'

The report recommended that water meters be installed and, although this did not happen in 1880, further attempts to do this occurred over the next 20 years. In 1901, the Ratepayers Association (RPA) was formed. This argued that water should be a right of existence, not a **commodity** to be sold.

In 1902, the city authorities again proposed to install water meters and to prosecute people if taps were found to be dripping on their property. A series of public meetings by the RPA were held. The issue was due to be debated by the Legislative Council on 23 March, at the Red House (seat of Parliament in the Republic of Trinidad and Tobago).

The burning of the Red House, Water Riots, 1903.

Protesters outside the Red House were angered to discover that they were not allowed into the public gallery. This situation was made worse when they were told that admission to the council chamber would be by ticket only. Some protesters began throwing stones at the Red House, while others broke into the building. The Red House was then set on fire and destroyed. When the police reacted to this, 16 people were killed.

A Commission of Enquiry found that:

- the government had acted in an unjust manner by not consulting the public about the proposals
- the lack of black representation on the Legislative Council was one of the causes of the riot
- water management fell under the remit of local, not national, government.

Following these findings, a black member of the RPA was appointed to the Legislative Council.

Exercise

3. In about 50 words, explain the background that led to the water riots in 1903.

4. Explain why the Commission of Enquiry found that the government had acted in an unjust manner.

Labour riots 1930 ▶▶

As the 1920s came to a close, there was considerable unrest in the labour market in Trinidad. Both internal and external factors contributed to this unrest, which resulted in the 1930 riots.

External factors included:

- After World War I, England and the USA reduced the amount of sugar they imported from Trinidad. Consequently, unemployment surged as England and the USA were Trinidad's main market.

- The soldiers who fought in World War I were ill-treated and discriminated against. They returned home embittered and ready for radical action.

- In 1929, the global economic depression after the Wall Street Crash led to inflation and food shortages.

- Garveyism encouraged persons of African descent to recognise their true worth and embrace their heritage. Through the formation of the United Negro Improvement Association (UNIA), persons of African descent were encouraged to establish an independent black economy and thereby improve their standard of living. These ideologies gained momentum by the 1935 Italian invasion of Ethiopia. It was the last African state to be colonised by European powers. This news was meet with defiance by Caribbean people, including the people of Trinidad and Tobago.

Internal factors included:

- Worsening economic conditions brought on by increased **inflation**.
- High unemployment.
- Low wages.
- Workers were subjected to poor working conditions. Managers extended tasks to maximise profits resulting in longer working hours and working on Sundays or public holidays with no extra pay. Nor was compensation offered for industrial accidents. Victimisation was rampant.
- Oppression of workers was rife and opposition to the government was stifled. The aftermath of the 1919–20 strikes illustrated this, as the government arrested and deported those who were involved in strikes and used ordinances such as the Strikes and Lockout Ordinance as weapons against dissension.

Marcus Mosiah Garvey (1887–1940), a black nationalist and Pan-Africanist.

Workers crushing cocoa beans with their feet.

- Trade union developments were restricted by the discrepancies in the law. For example, the law allowed for the registration of trade unions but failed to give them any protection or legalise peaceful protests.
- Infighting and internal conflict over the leadership in the Trinidad Workingmen's Association. Its members were dissatisfied with how their leader, Arthur Cipriani, represented them. Cipriani's leadership was marked by failure to bring about any changes related to wages or working conditions.

The impact of the 1930 riots

- Tubal Uriah Butler was arrested. He was released in 1946 after which he continued to speak up against racial discrimination, unemployment and inflation.
- The government accepted the recommendations of the Moyne and Foster Commission that, in order to quell further unrest and promote peaceful industrial relations, trade unions should be established along British lines.
- Greater cooperation between the British Trade Union Council and local trade unions was observed.
- The trade union movement expanded and new leaders emerged.
- The 1938 Trade Dispute Ordinance was enacted.
- The establishment of a Trade Union Congress in 1939.
- The Trade Union Ordinance was amended in 1939 to incorporate peaceful picketing and immunity from damages related to strikes.

Exercise

5. In your own words, summarise the causes of the 1930 labour riots

6. Name two impacts of the introduction of the 1939 trade union laws.

7. Find out more about Tubal Uriah Butler and create a timeline of the important dates in his life.

Project

Look back on Units 3.13–3.15. Imagine you are a mason, carpenter, railway worker, store clerk or oil worker working in Trinidad and Tobago in the 1920s and 1930s. In groups, role-play why you may be unhappy about your work. Create some slogans that could be used as protest banners about your work.

Members of the Communications Workers Union laying a wreath on the grave of Tubal Uriah Butler (1897–1977).

Activity

Imagine you were an oilfield worker in the 1930s in Trinidad. Write a brief report on why you took part in the 1930s riots.

Key vocabulary

commodity

inflation

The Black Power Movement

We are learning to:

- explain the causes and consequences of the Black Power Movement in Trinidad and Tobago
- list the individuals and groups involved in the Black Power Movement
- appreciate the motivation and struggles of the people and groups involved in the event
- present, using various media, issues connected to the movement.

Causes of the Black Power Movement in Trinidad ⟩⟩

At the start of the 1970s **Black Power** ideology swept across America and the Caribbean. In 1970, it took hold in Trinidad and Tobago. Although Trinidad and Tobago had been independent of British rule since 1962, the social and economic development of the nation had not progressed in the way that many had hoped:

The Black Power protests in the 1970s.

- Unemployment was at 12%, with 25% of youths being unemployed.
- Institutional racism remained in the workplace. In 1970, 53% of senior roles in companies employing over 100 people were held by white people.
- The 1965 Industrial Stabilization Act restricted workers' rights to protest and settle work grievances.
- Despite gaining independence and having a government headed by Eric Williams, there were still inequalities in society.
- Too many businesses in Trinidad and Tobago were not owned by local people, so their profits did not stay in the country.

In addition to this, Trinidadians were influenced by the American **Civil Rights Movement**, whose plan was to end discrimination against African Americans. They were also affected by the **Black Panther Party**, founded in America in 1966, whose aim was to secure better rights for the American black community.

Exercise

1. Explain briefly the origins of the Black Power Movement in Trinidad.

2. Why do you think were people attracted to the Black Power Movement?

Activity

Role-play the following scenario in pairs. It is 1970 and one of you is an activist preparing to go to a Black Power demonstration. Using the information on these two pages, decide why you are going to the protest. Your partner will be a television presenter, who will ask you why you think going to a demonstration will help the cause.

Consequences of the Black Power Movement in Trinidad

The Black Power Movement in Trinidad and Tobago was headed by Geddes Granger and Dave Darbeau of the National Joint Action Committee (NJAC) political party. George Weekes, President of the OGTU, supported them. The Black Power Movement in Trinidad and Tobago aimed to:

Black Power leader Geddes Granger addresses a huge crowd during demonstration early in March, 1970, Trinidad.

- end all injustice faced by people of colour in society
- ensure equal employment rights
- end foreign influence in the country
- improve the status of African culture in society.

Marches and demonstrations

In 1970, there were demonstrations against the government in several towns, attracting up to 50 000 people. Woodford Square in Port of Spain, renamed the People's Parliament, was packed with people at nightly meetings. When one demonstration turned violent, the army was called in, but two of its officers rebelled when they were told they may have to shoot protesters. On 21 April 1970, Eric Williams declared a **state of emergency** and the mutineers were arrested, tried in military courts and put in jail.

The consequences of the 1970 protests

The consequences of the protests of 1970 were:

- the emergence of black pride and consciousness
- new government economic policies to develop the economy and create jobs – the government had money to do this due to the increase in the price of oil in 1973; for example, the government bought companies such as Caroni (1975) Limited and invested in iron, steel and chemical industries, as well as improving infrastructure
- the slow end to discrimination against black people in the workplace and an increased awareness of injustice in Trinidadian society.

Activity

Using the internet, or newspaper articles given to you by your teacher, research the events of the Black Power Movement and act out its story.

Exercise

3. What were the aims of the Black Power Movement in Trinidad and Tobago?

4. In your own words, explain what happened in 1970, and the consequences.

Key vocabulary

Black Power

Civil Rights Movement

Black Panther Party

state of emergency

The West Indian Federation

We are learning to:

- outline the factors which led to the establishment of the Federation, its achievements and what contributed to its failure
- demonstrate an understanding of the values: loyalty, cooperation.

The formation of the West Indian Federation

The West Indian Federation was formed by 10 British colonies who wanted to put forward the idea of existing as a Federation, or separate entity, from the United Kingdom. Federation is the act of forming a political unity under a federal government. The idea was first put forward at a regional conference held in 1947 at Montego Bay, Jamaica, and the West Indies Federation came into being in 1958.

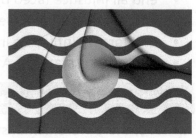
The flag of the West Indian Federation.

The motto of the West Indian Federation was 'To dwell together in unity.' This motto signified the Federation's aim of establishing an integrated community that would work together, cooperatively and loyally, as a single unit.

The aims of the Federation

The West Indian Federation had a number of aims.

- **Independence** – members wanted to achieve independence from Britain and they saw **regional unity** as a way of to do this. They also hoped this would prevent the United States from interfering in the Caribbean.
- Economic independence – much of the land and many of the businesses were owned by foreign companies.
- Free movement of people and goods – free movement around the islands of the West Indies. A new airline, British West Indies Airways, came into service, as well as two ships donated by Canada to improve transport between the islands.
- Goods prices – to get cheaper prices for imports and better prices for exports.
- Central planning – to allow economic development across the member states.

Although the Federation had failed, the idea of a unified body remained and organisations such as CARIFTA (1965) and CARICOM (1973) were later formed.

> **Did you know...?**
>
> The members of the West Indies Federation were:
>
> Antigua and Barbuda
>
> Barbados
>
> Dominica
>
> Grenada
>
> Jamaica
>
> Montserrat
>
> St Kitts-Nevis-Anguilla
>
> St Vincent and the Grenadines
>
> St Lucia
>
> Trinidad and Tobago.

The West Indies Federation lasted until 1962. It was disbanded when Jamaica and Trinidad and Tobago decided to leave the Federation. However, a number of reasons contributed to the collapse of the Federation.

Mary, Princess Royal and Governor Sir Solomon Hochoy were among the officials who attended the flag-raising ceremony at the Red House, to mark the independence of Trinidad and Tobago from the British Empire, August 1962.

- The Federation was weak – financially, it was not possible for the Federation to function together, as each state had its own economy.
- The aim of freedom of movement had not been achieved.
- Trinidad and Tobago and Jamaica were the biggest countries in the Federation and they were expected to bear most of the costs of the Federation. They thought this was unfair.
- The smaller countries feared that the more powerful countries would dominate the Federation.
- There was disagreement as to where the capital of the Federation should be.
- Jamaica objected to the colonial status of the Federation and felt that it was holding back true independence from Britain.
- The most respected leaders of the time preferred to remain as leaders in their own countries, rather than lead the Federation.

In September 1961, Jamaica held a referendum in which the people of Jamaica elected to pull out of the Federation.

Jamaica and Trinidad and Tobago became independent countries in 1962. The other countries in the Federation achieved independence later on.

Activity

Role-play a meeting of the West Indian Federation. There will need to be 10 in the group to represent the countries, and another person to chair the meeting. In your mock meeting, you could discuss how to make sure that people and goods can move freely between the countries, for example.

Exercise

1. In your own words, describe the aims of the West Indian Federation.

2. When was the Federation founded?

3. Name some of the achievements of the Federation.

4. In what year did the Federation disband?

5. Why did Jamaica and Trinidad and Tobago feel that their involvement disadvantaged them?

6. Why was it difficult for the Federation to function in financial terms?

7. True or false? The aim of freedom of movement had been achieved by the Federation.

8. What were the consequences of withdrawing from the Federation for Jamaica and Trinidad and Tobago?

Discussion

In groups, discuss whether it was a good or bad idea to disband the West Indian Federation.

Key vocabulary

independence

regional unity

Independence

We are learning to:

- define the following concepts: independence, patriotism, pride, national consciousness.

The road to independence

The collapse of the West Indian Federation in 1962 was the latest in a long line of events that paved the way for independence for Trinidad and Tobago:

- The ruling government (the PNM) in the period 1956–61 developed industry at home, rather than importing from abroad. This resulted in the growth of factories making clothes and household goods.
- The country was economically prosperous – the PNM encouraged the growth of the oil industry, cement-making plants, the fertiliser and petrochemical industries, and the construction and hotel industries.
- New primary and secondary schools had opened.
- There was harmony between the different cultures and races that made up the population, an increase in **national consciousness** of their shared heritage, and an increase in **patriotism** and **pride** for the nation.
- The PNM introduced a long-term plan for Tobago – to develop the electricity system, build new roads and hotels and extend the islands airstrip.

When the PNM won the 1961 general election, everything was in place to achieve independence. An Independence Constitution was drawn up, and after agreeing changes with the Democratic Labour Party (DLP), and then the British, Trinidad and Tobago finally achieved independence on 31 August 1962.

Following independence, some important changes took place:

- A **bicameral** legislature was set up, which consisted of a Senate and an elected House of Representatives.
- The Governor-General still represented the English crown, but this person was a citizen of Trinidad and Tobago.
- A new **constitution** was drawn up.
- The government had full control of all national and international matters and was allowed to make its own policies.

Dr Eric Williams speaking in London, around 1961.

Activity

Listen to the independence speech made by Dr Eric Williams. Summarise the main points of the speech – for example, the reasons he gives for independence. You could also convert the speech to a calypso and perform it in class.

Did you know...?

Our national flag is red, white and black. Red represents warmth, energy, courage and friendliness. White signifies purity, sincerity and the sea. Black stands for wealth, unity and strength.

Case study

Study this extract from the speech made over the radio on 31 August 1962 by the first Prime Minister, Dr Eric Williams.

Fellow Citizens,

It is a great honour to me to address this morning the citizens of the Independent Nation of Trinidad and Tobago as their first Prime Minister.

Your National Flag has been hoisted to the strains of your National Anthem, against the background of your National Coat of Arms, and amidst the beauty of your National Flower.

Your Parliament has been inaugurated by Her Royal Highness the Princess Royal, the representative of Her Majesty the Queen.

You have your own Governor General and your own Chief Justice, both appointed on the advice of your own Prime Minister. You have your own National Guard, however small.

You are now a member of the Commonwealth Family in your own right, equal in status to any other of its members. You hope soon to be a member of the World Family of Nations, playing your part, however insignificant, in world affairs.

You are on your own in a big world, in which you are one of many nations, some small, some medium size, some large. You are nobody's boss and nobody is your boss.

Questions

1. Which was the ruling party in Trinidad and Tobago at the time of independence?

2. Why was the economy of Trinidad and Tobago doing well in the period immediately before independence?

3. When was independence finally achieved?

4. What World Family of Nations do you think Dr Williams was referring to in his speech?

5. Do you think people found this speech moving? How do you think they felt when they heard it?

6. What do you think Dr Williams meant by 'You are nobody's boss and nobody is your boss.'

Dr Eric Williams arrives for a conference in London, around 1962.

Activity

Your teacher will play you some calypsos about the period, such as 'Independence Calypso' by Lord Brynner.

Key vocabulary

national consciousness

patriotism

pride

bicameral

constitution

Figures of the independence movement

We are learning to:

- explain the contribution of key figures to the independence movement
- appreciate the values of leadership, perseverance, duty, self-discipline.

Significant personalities of the independence period

There were a number of people who made a significant contribution to independence for Trinidad and Tobago.

Profile

Dr Eric Eustace Williams (1911–81)

Dr Eric Williams played the most significant role in the process of independence. Williams was educated at Queen's Royal College in Port of Spain. He won a scholarship and went to read history at Oxford University in the UK, where he graduated with a First in History in 1935. He returned to Trinidad in 1948.

In 1956, he founded the People's National Movement (PNM) and in the general election that year the PNM won 13 of the 24 available seats. The PNM was the first party government in Trinidad and Tobago, and Williams was appointed its first leader.

Williams recognised the need for a political party that stood for self-government, economic development, unity between races and the political education of the people. He also attacked racial inequality, the plantation system and political backwardness. He was a firm believer of democracy.

In 1962, Williams became the first Prime Minister of Trinidad and Tobago. He served from 1962 until he died in 1981. It was only through Williams's **perseverance, leadership** and **discipline** that he succeeded in his quest for independence.

Dr Eric Williams arrives for the Commonwealth Conference, 1962.

Exercise

1. What contributions did Dr Eric Williams make to Trinidad and Tobago?
2. In which year did Dr Williams found the PNM?
3. What were the policies that the PNM stood for?
4. In which year did the PNM form their first government?

Profile

Rudranath Capildeo (1920–70)

Rudranath Capildeo was Indo-Trinidadian. He was the leader of the Democratic Labour Party (DLP) from 1960 to 1969 and Leader of the Opposition in Parliament from 1961 to 1963. Capildeo was also an eminent mathematician.

The DLP was formed when three opposition parties in the Legislative Council joined together – the People's Democratic Party, the Trinidad Labour Party and the Party of Political Progress Groups.

Capildeo was asked to become the leader of the DLP when members of the DLP could not agree with each other. As Capildeo was a scientist with a good reputation, they thought he could oppose Eric Williams as an intellectual equal.

In 1963, he accepted a senior post at the University of London and tried to run the DLP while in London. Despite unrest in the party about his role, Capildeo continued to be leader of the party though he was only able to dedicate time to the party during summer months and during the general elections of 1961 and 1966. After defeat in the 1966, he was finally removed as the party leader in 1969.

Capildeo's greatest **duty** for the nation of Trinidad and Tobago was reviewing the Independence Constitution in 1962 and suggesting a number of changes (which were adopted). He was also responsible for making sure that the freedom of worship formed part of the Trinidad and Tobago constitution.

Profile

Albert Gomes (1911–78)

Gomes was the founder of the Federated Workers Trade Union in 1937, and held a number of public offices, including on Port of Spain city council (1938–47) and Member of Parliament (1958–61). He was known for campaigning to end the censorship of calypso – achieved in 1951 – and for championing workers' rights and challenging authority.

Project

Your teacher will ask you to complete a class exhibition about Trinidad and Tobago's independence. Include the following: the key people involved, a timeline of events, plus photographs and drawings.

Exercise

5. What contribution did Rudranath Capildeo make to Trinidad and Tobago?

6. Outline Albert Gomes' contribution to Trinidad and Tobago.

Key vocabulary

perseverance

leadership

discipline

duty

Questions

See how well you have understood the topics in this unit.

1. Match the key vocabulary word (i–vii) with its definition (a–g).

   i) first peoples
   ii) indigenous
   iii) annex/annexation
   iv) integrated
   v) diversify
   vi) constitutional reform
   vii) semi-autonomous

   a) joined together or working cooperatively as a single unit
   b) the first known population of a place, usually indigenous people
   c) changing the laws and policies by which a state is governed
   d) originally present in a place; living there naturally; not imported from another place
   e) partly independent or self-governing
   f) take over land from another country
   g) enlarge or expand a range of products, operations or industries

2. Why was only a small percentage of the population allowed to vote for deputies of the Legislative Council and Assembly of Tobago?

3. What products helped to make Tobago a prosperous island?

4. What does ward of Trinidad mean?

5. Create your own timeline of the 'changing hands' of Tobago.

6. What did Audrey Jeffers achieve in 1936?

7. Who was Clothil Walcott and what was her contribution to Trinidad?

8. Write a reflective diary entry of a Trinidadian travelling to Tobago in the 19th century. Note down the differences and similarities between the islands during this period.

9. Use the internet to research the biography of one of the people involved in the Black Power Movement – Geddes Granger, Dave Darbeau or George Weekes. Write about 150 words, and include any photos you can find.

10. Why was Eric Williams the first Prime Minister of Trinidad and Tobago?

11. Consider two perspectives on the union of Tobago with Trinidad, and create them as a reflective diary entry.

12. Name the party that Rudranath Capildeo founded and the year in which he did so.

13. What three other political parties did Capildeo's party form from?

14. Match the dates (i–vi) with the events (a–f) in the history of Tobago.

   i) 1608–28 onwards
   ii) 1620s–1630s
   iii) 1642–81
   iv) 1684–1762
   v) 1814
   vi) 1876

   a) The Dutch claim ownership
   b) Becomes a British Crown Colony
   c) The British claim ownership
   d) Duchy of Courland has a settlement
   e) Britain formally gains control of the island
   f) Tobago is declared neutral

15. In around 150 words, write a newspaper account of the Arena Massacre.

16. Write a report outlining the arguments for and against the West Indian Federation. Write about 150 words.

17. Explain what the metayage system is.

18. Explain the role of James Biggart, A.N.R. Robinson and A.P.T James in the history of Trinidad and Tobago.

19. Write a reflective piece expressing what the independence of Trinidad and Tobago means to you. Use around 100 words.

20. Use primary and secondary sources to research the decline of the sugar industry in the late 19th century in Trinidad and Tobago. Write about 200 words. Add photos from magazines, the internet or your own drawings.

21. What does the word 'secession' mean? Do you think that Tobago would benefit from secession from Trinidad? Give reasons for your answer.

22. What contribution do you think T.U.B. Butler made to Trinidad and Tobago.

23. Using primary and secondary sources, research Elma Francois and the NWCSA. Examine her contribution to the trade union movement and the fight for social justice in Trinidad and Tobago.

Checking your progress

To make good progress in understanding different aspects of the history of your country, check to make sure you understand these ideas.

Explain the presence of the indigenous people of Trinidad and Tobago.

Understand the history of Tobago, pre-1492 to the present day.

Use primary and secondary sources to research aspects of the history of Trinidad and Tobago.

Explain the contribution of key figures in trade unionism and social activism.

Explain the contribution of key groups in trade unionism and social activism.

Use a graphic organiser to compile the key events in the history of the TWA and OWTU.

Explain the causes and consequences of the Black Power Movement in Trinidad and Tobago.

Explore the aims of the Black Power Movement in Trinidad and Tobago.

Research the events of the Black Power movement.

Explain the aims of the West Indian Federation.

Understand how Trinidad and Tobago reached independence.

Write about what the independence of Trinidad and Tobago means to you.

Glossary

abolish/abolished when a system has been put to an end

adult suffrage the right of adults to vote in an election

Amerindians the native people of America

ancestral lineage parents, grandparents, great grandparents, great-great grandparents and so on

Anglicanism a Protestant denomination: Anglicans believe they follow a 'middle way' between Catholicism and Protestantism

annex/annexation taking over land from another country

apprenticeship someone who works for someone else learning a skill: the apprenticeship scheme was for formerly enslaved people who had to serve their former owners free of charge for 40.5 hours a week for 4-6 years; they were to be paid for any extra hours that they worked

Arawaks the Taino tribe, Amerindian settlers in Trinidad and Tobago

artefact an object that is historically or culturally interesting

bibliography a list of the sources (usually secondary sources) that you consulted when doing research

bicameral two houses or chambers in a government

Black Panther Party civil rights movement founded in America in 1966, whose aim was to secure better rights for the American Black community

Black Power a name used by African Americans in the USA to describe a movement that aimed to achieve self-determination for people of African/black descent

Caribs the Kalinago tribe, Amerindian settlers in Trinidad and Tobago

century a period of 100 years

Civil Rights Movement a mass protest movement that started in the United States in the 1960s, which was against racial discrimination

class the division of people in a society into groups according to their social status, for example upper class, middle class and working class

collective bargaining negotiation between one or more trade unions and one or more employers

colonialism gaining control over land in another country and exploiting its wealth

commodity something which can be sold for money

community the people with whom you live and work

constitution the principles and laws by which a country is governed

cooperatively working helpfully with others

Crown Colony a country ruled by the monarch of another country

cultural diversity a wide range of customs, traditions and beliefs in a society

curriculum (curricula) the syllabus; the subjects you learn about at school

customs a way of behaviour that has been established for a long time

decade a period of 10 years

democracy a system of government in which a country's citizens choose their rulers by voting for them in elections

democratically government of the people, by the people, for the people, through their elected representatives

denomination a group having a distinctive interpretation of Christianity

differences specific instances of being unalike

digital storytelling being filmed as you tell your story

discipline when someone is able to behave in a controlled way

discrimination unfair treatment of a person based on race, origin, colour, religion or sex

diversification increasing and varying the types of something; for example, farming and agriculture practices

diversify to enlarge or expand a range of products, operations or industries

documents formal written information

duty something that you have to do, for example in your job, or your school work

emancipation being freed from slavery or the removal of restraints or restrictions on an individual or group of people

enslaved people people who had no physical, social, political or economic rights or freedom

established to set up or to start up

Executive Arm where the agreed policies of the Legislative Arm of the Tobago House of Assembly are carried out

exploit to use resources or raw materials for commercial gain

extra-curricular a subject not normally part of the usual school or college courses

family tree a tree-like diagram that shows the ancestry of a family

fertilisers chemicals that promote fast plant growth

first people the first known population of a place, usually indigenous people

formerly enslaved people people who were enslaved and were emancipated or freed

free trade trade which allows people to buy and sell goods freely, without restrictions

future something that may or will occur

gender equality equal treatment, opportunities and rights for men and women

generation a period of around 25–30 years

governor an official who is appointed to govern a country

Hinduism the more common name for the followers of Sanatan Dharma who believe that there is a universal soul called Brahman; this universal soul can take the form of many gods and goddesses

historical site a place that has special historic, cultural or social value, usually protected by law in order to preserve it

House of Assembly the body which is responsible for local government in Tobago and which also have some national government functions

immigrant a person who has moved from their country to live and work in another country; that person may opt to live there permanently

immigration the migration of a person or group of people into a country where they were not born in order to settle or reside there

indentured/indentureship contract labour with harsh conditions

independence being able to do things without assistance or direction

indigenous originally present in a place; living there naturally; not imported from another place

inflation increase in prices over time

inhumane extreme cruelty

internal migration when a person moves within the same country

Islam a religion which originated in what is now Saudi Arabia, based on the revelations of the Prophet Muhammad; followers of Islam are known as Muslims

kinship the members of your immediate family

landmark a building or a feature which is easily noticed

leadership when a leader (or leaders) influences a group to achieve a common objective

legacy something handed down to future generations, or received from an ancestor or predecessor

Legislative Arm where policy is made in the Tobago House of Assembly

Legislative Council established by the British Government to run Trinidad it was made up of a Governor, the Chief Justice, the Colonial Treasurer, and Protector of Slaves

majority/ruling party the party that gets the most votes in an election and is therefore able to lead the government

metayage system a form of sharecropping, in which the metayer (sharecropper) occupied a piece of land on which he/she planted cane

Methodism a Protestant denomination based on the teachings of a Christian teacher called John Wesley; this denomination emphasises helping the poor and working to serve the community

migrated to have moved from one place to another

migration the temporary or permanent movement of people from one place to another; reasons can include 'pull factors' such as for work, education and change of location

mission definition of the aims or goals of an organisation or institution

missionaries someone who has been sent to another country to teach about Christianity

monoculture where a country uses most of its agricultural land to plant one main crop on a large scale

Moravian a Protestant denomination from Germany: one of the oldest Protestant denominations, it has a long tradition of missionary work in the Caribbean

multicultural society a society consisting of many cultures

mutiny a rebellion against authority, usually involving military personnel against their superior officers

national consciousness a shared sense of national identity

nationalist connected with the desire of a group of people within a country for political independence

next of kin your closest living relatives

oath of allegiance to swear loyalty or commitment to someone or something

oral source where information is passed on by the spoken word of a person about their earlier life's experiences or events that they witnessed

oral tradition where information is passed from generation to generation through the spoken word

override to cancel someone else's decision

past events that happened before the present time

patriotism showing a deep love for, and devotion to, your country

peasant farming the small-scale rearing of livestock, growing of vegetables and ground provisions, and the cultivation of crops such as corn, cocoa and bananas, primarily for consumption by the farmer and their family, with any remaining produce able to be sold at market

perseverance when someone continues to do something, even if it is difficult to achieve

personal history the history of the people from whom you are descended (your ancestors) and the people to whom you are related

place of birth where you were born

political franchise suffrage, the right to vote in an election

political suffrage the right to vote in political elections

Presbyterianism a Protestant denomination: Presbyterians follow a version of Christianity that originated in the 1500s with a teacher called John Calvin

present something that exists or is happening now

pride a sense of respect you have for your country

primary source a document or object created at the time of an event

principles basic ideas or rules that explain or control how something happens or works

Protestantism/protestant a branch of Christianity that moved away from some of the traditions of the Catholic church/a person who practices protestantism

public school government school

race groups into which human beings can be divided into according to their physical features, such as the colour of their skin

racial diversity when people from many different backgrounds make up a population

rationale the reasons or intentions for someone to do something

regional unity cooperation and working together by people who live in a certain area

religion a system of beliefs and practices shared by a group of people

Roman Catholicism the original organised form of Christianity, which remained unchanged for over 1000 years

rural places which are located in the countryside, away from towns and cities

secession when a country, or a group, separates from a larger group

secondary source a document created after an event took place

secular non-religious; not following a religion

semi-autonomous partly independent or self-governing

similarities things that are the same in some ways

slavery people who are the property of another person and have to work for that person

social activism to campaign for better social conditions in society

social justice fairness in society

social militancy to bring about social change by confrontational means

source (history) documents and written texts where we learn about history

state of emergency a time when the government suspends normal constitutional procedures because of a national danger or disaster

trade union an organised group of workers which protects their interests and rights

traditional following the customs or ways of behaving that have continued in a group of people or society for a long time without changing

traditions beliefs, behaviours and actions that people hand down from one generation to the next

transatlantic slave trade the buying and selling of enslaved people, specifically involving the forced removal of African people from their homeland and their transportation to the Caribbean, to work predominantly on sugar plantations

unification the process where two countries, or more, join together

uniform set of clothes for the members of an organisation, such as schoolchildren or scouts

urban belonging to a town or a city

village a settlement of between a few hundred and a few thousand people, or a small community in a country area

vision planning for the future in an imaginative and creative way

ward an administrative part of a country or a smaller division within a country used for voting purposes

ward school government school in a ward (district)

working class the group of people in a society whose work usually involves physical skills, who do not own much property and who have a relatively low social status

Index

Acknowledgements

The publishers wish to thank the following for permission to reproduce photographs.
Every effort has been made to trace copyright holders and to obtain their permission for
the use of copyright materials. The publishers will gladly receive any information enabling
them to rectify any error or omission at the first opportunity.

(T = top, B = bottom)

p. 8 Archive Farms/Getty Images; p. 10
Marzolino/Shutterstock; p. 11 Steven Wright/
Shutterstock; p.12 Wavebreak media/
Shutterstock; p. 15 Topical Press Agency/
stringer/Getty Images; p. 16 tbkmedia.de/
Alamy; p. 19 Gordon Brooks/AFP/Getty
Images; p. 20 Anton_Ivanov/Shutterstock;
p. 20 SEAN DRAKES / Alamy Stock Photo;
p. 20 Pete Niesen/Shutterstock; p. 22 Clive
Tully/Alamy; p. 23 Art Directors & TRIP/Alamy;
p. 24 Fox Photos/Getty Images; p. 33 Interfoto/
Alamy Stock Photo; p. 35 Morphart Creation/
Shutterstock; p. 37 Public Domain; p. 38
Print Collecto/Hulton Archive/Getty Images;
p. 40 Heritage Images/Hulton Archive/Getty
Images; p. 42T Stefano Bianchetti/Contributor/
Getty Images; p. 42B Natt.Gov; p. 43 Steven
Wright/Shutterstock; p. 44T LatitudeStock/
Alamy Stock Photo; p. 44B Anton_Ivanov/
Shutterstock; p. 46 Tom Hanslien Photography/
Alamy Stock Photo; p. 49 Print Collector/
Corbis Historical/ Contributor/Getty Images;
p. 50 Leiden University Library/Public Domain;
p. 52 Mara Vivat/Corbis Historical/Getty
Images; p. 53 Bettmann/Contributor/Getty
Images; p. 56 EyesWideOpen/Contributor/
Getty Images; p. 57 Sean Drakes/CON/
Contributor/Getty Images; p. 58 Altin Osmanaj/
Alamy Stock Photo; p. 59 John de la Bastide/
Shutterstock.com; p. 60 Hulton Archive/
Stringer/Getty Images; p. 62 Tamarin60/
Shutterstock; p. 70 Marekuliasz/Shutterstock;
p. 72 Ann Ronan Pictures/Print Collector/
Getty Images; p. 75 Robert Down/Alamy Stock
Photo; p. 76 Print Collector/Corbis Historical/
Contributor/Getty Images;; p. 78 INTERFOTO/
Alamy Stock Photo; p. 79 Ian Brierley/
LatitudeStock/ Alamy Stock Photo;
p. 80 North Wind Picture Archives/Alamy Stock
Photo; p. 82 Archive Farms/Getty Images; p.
83 Art Directors & TRIP/Alamy Stock Photo;
p. 84 Sean Drakes/LatinContent/Getty Images;
p. 88 John de la Bastide/Alamy Stock Photo; p.
89 Glyn Thomas/Alamy Stock Photo;
p. 90 Hulton Archive/Getty Images; p. 91 Sean
Drakes/Alamy Stock Photo; p. 92 Hulton-
Deutsch Collection/CORBIS/Getty Images;
p. 93 Lefteris Papaulakis/Shutterstock; p. 94
dbimages/Alamy Stock Photo; p. 96 University
of the West Indies; p. 97 public domain; p. 98
Science History Images / Alamy Stock Photo;
p. 98 D and S Photography Archives / Alamy
Stock Photo; p. 99 REUTERS / Alamy Stock
Photo; p. 100 AP Image; p. 101 Bettmann/
Contributor/Getty Images; p. 102 yui/
Shutterstock; p. 103 Keystone/Hulton Archive/
Getty Images; p. 104 Val Wilmer/Getty Images;
p. 105 Popperfoto/Getty Images; p. 106
Bentley Archive/Popperfoto/Getty Images.